Cultural Functions of Translation

Multilingual Matters

About Translation
  PETER NEWMARK
Annotated Texts for Translation: French – English
  BEVERLY ADAB
Annotated Texts for Translation: English – French
  BEVERLY ADAB
Linguistic Auditing
  NIGEL REEVES and COLIN WRIGHT
Paragraphs on Translation
  PETER NEWMARK
Practical Guide for Translators
  GEOFFREY SAMUELSSON-BROWN
The Coming Industry of Teletranslation
  MINAKO O'HAGAN
Translation, Power, Subversion
  R. ALVAREZ and M.C.-A. VIDAL (eds)

Please contact us for the latest book information:
Multilingual Matters Ltd, Frankfurt Lodge, Clevedon Hall,
Victoria Road, Clevedon, Avon BS21 7SJ, England

Cultural Functions of Translation

Edited by
Christina Schäffner and
Helen Kelly-Holmes

MULTILINGUAL MATTERS LTD
Clevedon • Philadelphia • Adelaide

Library of Congress Cataloging in Publication Data

Cultural Functions of Translation/Edited by Christina Schäffner and Helen Kelly-Holmes
Also published as Vol. 1, No. 3 of *Current Issues in Language and Society*.
1. Translating and interpreting–Social aspects. 2. Language and culture. 3. Inter-cultural communication. I. Schäffner, Christina. II. Kelly-Holmes, Helen, 1968-
P306.2.C85   1995
418'.02–dc20   95-42194

British Library Cataloguing in Publication Data

A CIP catalogue record for this book is available from the British Library.

ISBN 1-85359-333-8 (hbk)

Multilingual Matters Ltd

UK: Frankfurt Lodge, Clevedon Hall, Victoria Road, Clevedon, Avon BS21 7SJ.
USA: 1900 Frost Road, Suite 101, Bristol, PA 19007, USA.
Australia: P.O. Box 6025, 83 Gilles Street, Adelaide, SA 5000, Australia.

Printed and bound in Great Britain by Short Run Press.

CONTENTS

EDITORIAL

Christina Schäffner

*Institute for the Study of Language and Society, Aston University,
Aston Triangle, Birmingham B4 7ET*

Culture in Translation and Translation Studies

Throughout the centuries, translations have contributed to the processing and exchange of information both within and across cultural boundaries. Translating as an activity is almost as old as mankind, but the more systematic occupation with this phenomenon — dealing with translation as an academic and scholarly endeavour and deriving consequences for translation training — is relatively new. Although there are statements about methods of translating that date from the Middle Ages (for example, Martin Luther's comments on how he translated the Bible, cf. Störig, 1963), they were not based on a particular theory of translation. Attempts to develop a more theoretical account of translation began in the 1950s. The developments of these accounts are a reflection of both the dominant scientific paradigms of the time and the development of linguistics. But even today, translation studies has not become a homogeneous discipline.

Translation has traditionally been described as a comparative linguistic undertaking, whereby translation has been approached primarily from the perspective of the differences in language structures. But this has turned out to be too narrow a view. As Nida (1994: 1) says: 'It is true that in all translating and interpreting the source and target languages must be implicitly or explicitly compared, but all such interlingual communication extends far beyond the mechanics of linguistic similarities and contrasts.' One of the main reasons for this is that 'the meaning of verbal symbols on any and every level depends on the culture of the language community. Language is a part of culture, and in fact, it is the most complex set of habits that any culture exhibits. Language reflects the culture, provides access to the culture, and in many respects constitutes a model of the culture' (Nida, 1994: 1).

Recently, therefore, the need for treating translation from a wide range of perspectives has been recognised (e.g. Snell-Hornby, 1988). Translating and interpreting are essentially communicative processes that produce texts. The important features of sociological settings have been included, and it has been recognised that, apart from linguistics, insights from a number of scientific disciplines, for example psychology, cultural anthropology, and communication theory should be employed to explain the complex phenomenon of translation.

What happens in this complex process? A target text is produced that is based on a source text (Neubert, 1985: 18 speaks of translation as 'source-text-induced target-text-production'). This target-text-production may be initiated in the source or in the target culture. Both source text and target text fulfil a specific function, play a specific role in their respective language communities and cultures. The source text was produced in a source culture, it is a product of this

1

culture (which is itself heterogeneous), and it functioned in that culture. The target text has to function in a new culture. Apart from the two cultures usually being different, the functions of the texts may be different as well. The function of an instruction manual or a scientific article will usually be the same for the source and the target text, namely instructing and informing, respectively. However, a speech by a politician at an electioneering rally may have a persuasive function in the source culture, but only an informative function when translated for a target culture (that is to say, members of the target culture are not expected to cast their votes for this politician).

Translation and Cultural Identities

The function of a text may also be seen in a wider, social context, that is, how a text effects the structure and functioning of a society. For example, a source text can consolidate or challenge existing power structures in its source culture. Translations, too, may have far-reaching effects in the target culture. Such effects may result from the picture of the source culture that translations present for the target culture. Where does knowledge about cultures usually come from, including knowledge that other cultures may be different? Such knowledge can be acquired by living in the other culture, by watching undubbed films, or by reading texts produced in this culture — but all this obviously requires knowledge of the language of this culture. The other way of gaining knowledge of other cultures is through translations. These translations stand for the original: they replace it. Translation as a 'culture transcending process' (Vermeer, 1992: 40) is thus an important way of forming cultural identities and of positioning cultures.

These aspects are the topics of this issue of *Current Issues in Language and Society*. It is based on papers given by two scholars from the United States of America and Canada in the winter of 1994/95. Lawrence Venuti discusses the role of translation for the formation of cultural identities, and Candace Séguinot focuses on the effects of globalisation for translating advertising.

The effects which translated texts have in the target culture are determined by the choice to translate a text and publish it, and also by the way in which these texts are read, comprehended, reviewed, and made use of in social, cultural, and institutional settings. All of these factors play an important role in the formation of cultural identities, the topic of Lawrence Venuti's paper. His main aim is to show that translation wields enormous power in constructing representations of foreign cultures. Translation can create stereotypes for foreign countries that reflect domestic cultural and political values and they can be instrumental in shaping domestic attitudes towards foreign countries.

Venuti discusses conservative or transgressive effects of a translation. By examining several translation projects from different periods he shows 'how translation forms particular cultural identities and maintains them with a relative degree of coherence and homogeneity'. His examples fall into the broad category of literary texts — novels, philosophical and religious texts. Venuti argues that American publishers established an ethnocentric canon of Japanese fiction in

English that was based on a well-defined stereotype, a representation that reflected a domestic nostalgia for an exotic pre-war Japan.

The example for a philosophical text is Jones's existentialist-informed translation of Aristotle's 'Poetics' which displaced the dominant academic reading and acquired an institutional authority. The controversies surrounding the translation of the Bible in the early Christian Church, for example Jerome's project of translating the Old Testament, show that translations may bring about social change by revising ideological qualifications and thereby modifying institutional roles or functions.

Venuti also considers how translation creates possibilities for cultural resistance, innovation, and change. He argues in his preliminary comments that 'any agenda of cultural resistance for translation must take specifically cultural forms, must choose foreign texts and translation methods that deviate from the canonical or dominant ones.' Translation should, where appropriate, reveal and accentuate difference.

The identity-forming power of translation is also evident in non-literary texts. Candace Séguinot discusses the specific case of advertising, which is an all-invasive aspect of our daily lives. Advertisements may promote a product (usually with a view to immediate purchase) or a service, and usually the visual element — which can be in an iconic, symbolic or indexical relationship with the product — is of key importance. Ads invest the products with a very special significance for the consumer. When the products are foreign, the advertising and marketing campaign must establish this significance of the product. Sometimes products are closely identified with their culture of origin, they may indeed reinforce stereotypical images of this culture. But they can also lead to a revision of that stereotype and an establishment of a culture-independent, or supra-national identity associated with a product.

Translators are expected to take responsibility for the final form of an ad, and Séguinot argues that 'the marketing of goods and services across cultural boundaries involves an understanding of culture and semiotics that goes well beyond both language and design.' Her examples illustrate how cultural differences affect marketing. In translating ads, an almost literal translation is inadequate in creating an appeal to a different target audience. Conceptual transfer from source culture to different target cultures can also be full of pitfalls, because of differences in national perceptions and preferences.

In discussing advertising, another important factor is introduced, namely that through translations, new international or supranational cultures may emerge. This is termed 'globalisation', and various aspects would come under this heading. Globalisation of the translation business sometimes means also providing full marketing services in addition to translation and interpretation. It may also involve devising different local campaigns or developing one common, international or supranational marketing and advertising campaign. And in a world of global communication, some groups, for example adolescents and business travellers the world over, form a common market across cultures.

Translation Strategies

Both papers make it absolutely clear that translation is not a matter of words only, but that it is a matter of making intelligible a whole culture. One of the key concepts in both papers is the idea of translation strategies.

Since translation studies is not a homogeneous discipline, as said above, it is only logical that some terms are used differently, or even controversially. One of the most controversial terms is the term *equivalence*. Other key concepts that are differently used are *strategy* and *function*, and this divergence also becomes obvious in the debates.

Venuti differentiates between foreignising and domesticating as his two main strategies. These two strategies can be found especially in the translation of literary texts. Domesticating means bringing the foreign culture closer to the reader in the target culture, making the text recognisable and familiar. Foreignising, on the other hand, means taking the reader over to the foreign culture, making him or her see the (cultural and linguistic) differences. Venuti (1994) argues that in domesticating foreign texts, translators were in fact maintaining the literary standards of the social elite while constructing cultural identities for their nations on the basis of (archaic) foreign cultures. A foreignising strategy seeks to evoke a sense of the foreign. This strategy necessarily answers to a domestic situation, where it may be designed to serve a cultural and political agenda. Macura (1990), for example, has shown that 19th century Czech culture virtually 'cloned' itself on the German model, and that translation thus actually 'constituted' a culture.

Of course, the culture to which the translator belongs is also important. Venuti's discussion usually assumes the translator to be a member of the target culture: only in these circumstances is the distinction between foreignising and domesticating translation strategies clearly understandable. That is, the translator is a member of the domestic society for which the source culture is foreign, is the 'other'.

In his preliminary remarks, Venuti complains that 'the fact of translation is erased by suppressing the linguistic and cultural differences of the foreign text, assimilating it to dominant values in the target-language culture, making it recognisable and therefore seemingly untranslated. With this domestication the translated text passes for the original'. However, these critical remarks would have to be relativised. The role of the text type, the genre, as well as the purpose of the target text are factors that decisively influence the final linguistic form and the lay-out of the target text. A distinction can be made between more or less conventionalised text types that exist in both cultures, and text types which are introduced into the target culture only through translation, for example Bible translations that gave many languages their first written form. In the case of translating text types that are highly conventionalised, the conventions of the target culture have to be taken into account, because in these cases the target addressees expect to read a text in a recognisable, familiar form. A case in point would be instruction manuals, for which domestication would be the only effective strategy (unless the purpose, the skopos of the target text, is to show what the source text looks like). Technical or legal texts too, often respond in a relatively predictable way to a series of conventional norms. On the other hand, literary texts, as a rule, do not conform strictly to predictable norms and conventions — and it is mainly with reference to literary texts that foreignisation versus domestication has traditionally been discussed (cf. Schleiermacher, 1838; and also Weck, 1876 who said: 'So steht denn der Übersetzer mitten inne zwischen zwei Forderungen, die zu versöhnen fast unmöglich erscheint. Auf der einen Seite ruft ihm der Dichter zu: habe Ehrfurcht vor meinem Eigentum; nimm mir nichts, aber schiebe mir auch nichts unter! Auf der anderen Seite verlangt das Publikum: habe Achtung vor meinem Geschmack; bringe mir nichts, als was mir gefällt und wie es mir gefällt!' [The translator is in the middle of two demands that seem almost impossible to reconcile. On one side, the author calls out to him: respect my property, don't take anything away from me, and don't attribute anything falsely to me. On the other side, the audience demands: respect our taste, give us only what we like and how we like it].

Séguinot's concept of strategies is a wider one, as can be seen in her discussion of the factors translators have to take into account, factors such as understanding constraints by the form and functions of the source text, interpreting the visual means, understanding the underlying object or concept, and how to react when there is no access to the product.

The term translation strategy is also often used synonymously with translation principle, translation method or translation technique. Categories here may be literal versus free translation, or principle of transparent translation versus principle of equal effect of source text and target text. The treatment of specific translation problems, for example how to deal with wordplays or ambiguity, how to translate proper names, how to translate metaphors, or how to overcome lexical gaps, are also sometimes discussed under the heading of translation strategies, although the term translation technique might be more appropriate.

The question of how one should translate has been asked again and again, and it has been answered differently in the literature. Savory (1968: 54) has summarised the seemingly contradictory alternative demands made of translation and stated them in the form of simple juxtapositions:

(1) A translation must give the words of the original.
(2) A translation must give the ideas of the original.
(3) A translation should read like an original work.
(4) A translation should read like a translation.
(5) A translation should reflect the style of the original.
(6) A translation should possess the style of the translation.
(7) A translation should read as a contemporary of the original.
(8) A translation should read as a contemporary of the translation.
(9) A translation may add to or omit from the original.
(10) A translation may never add to or omit from the original.
(11) A translation of verse should be in prose.
(12) A translation of verse should be in verse.

A strategy may best be seen as the idea of an agent about the best way to act in order to reach a goal. This overall goal will dominate a number of lower level, more detailed, decisions and actions. As soon as we ask what the purpose of a translation is, and who it is for, reformulation, paraphrase, textual explication, and so on, come in naturally as part of translation (cf. Schäffner & Herting, 1994).

The Role of Translators and Translation Ethics

In her discussion of the translation of advertising, Séguinot raises a number of points that relate to questions such as: What do translators have to know? Which activities are truly translational activities, and which ones are outside the realm of a translator's work? Where can we draw a line? This becomes especially obvious in the field of translating advertising, which seems to be a borderline case between translation and marketing.

Both Venuti and Séguinot stress the fact that translators should have knowledge of the foreign language and the culture. Only then can they successfully realise their role as interlingual and intercultural mediators. Séguinot points out that in a changing world, the boundaries of knowledge needed by the profession are also changing. She presents a number of points a translator should know which have not traditionally been seen as specific tasks of a translator. These points are that translators need to understand the basics of marketing and legal jurisdictions; they should know that many cultures have taboos concerning references to sex and alcohol, and they should be aware of standardisations or regulations.

When all such aspects are included in translation, a theoretical consequence would be that for explaining this phenomenon it would not be necessary to make a distinction between translation and adaptation. Being aware of what is expected of translators will also have consequences for translator training — a topic which was discussed at length at one of the two CILS seminars. Translators cannot obviously be prepared for each individual translation problem they may have to face. But what can be taught are generalisable translation strategies and translation techniques. Strategies have to do with problem-solving and decision-making. Decision-making in translation is largely subject to normative constraints resulting from text-type conventions or norms within the target culture. Such norms can be taught and learned and put to use. In addition, translators have to be aware of the fact that cultures not only express ideas differently, but they also shape concepts and texts differently.

The translator, as the expert communicator, is 'at the crucial centre of a long chain of communication from original initiator to ultimate receiver of a message: a human link across a cultural frontier' (Chesterman, 1993: 74). This metaphor also stresses the ethical responsibility of the translator, an aspect that is of particular relevance for both papers.

Traditore traduttore — the translator as the traitor — is one of the most often used clichés in translation. But translators have an important role to play, for example as 'rewriters' of works of literature. The German writer Günter Grass gives a convincing example of how translators are not traitors to the original authors but a vital link, in that they play an important role in taking texts to a wider audience. He reports about week-long meetings with translators who were to translate his novels 'The Flounder' and 'Meeting at Telgte':

I have never been so thoroughly, painstakingly, precisely and rigorously wrung out as I was by my translators. They … met … with the author to go over 'The Flounder' line by line. What I should have known now became abundantly clear to me: translators are the keenest of readers. They discover all the author's tricks, notice when he cheats and are aware of his absurdities. (Grass, 1984: 19)

In the context of conservative versus transgressive effects of translations and of ethics in translation, Venuti introduces the concepts of ethnocentric and non-ethnocentric translation. He is very much in favour of the latter since it promises 'a greater openness to cultural differences, whether they are located abroad or at home [and] they may [thus] well be worth the risks.'

Séguinot speaks out against restricting the responsibilities of the translator and advocates taking on a managerial role when she says at the end of her paper: 'Going global successfully means taking control of the final product, researching the cultural and marketing aspects, and making sure the translation conforms to the legal constraints.'

An ethics of translation means first of all that translators, that is, *all* translators, not only translators of literary texts or advertising, take responsibility for their actions, and that they have to be trained and equipped to be able to do so. Only then will the role and the status of the translator and of translation studies as an academic discipline be fully recognised in society.

Jakob Grimm compared translation to crossing a river, which works nicely in German because of the polysemy (über*setzen* = translate, *über*setzen = cross the river):

Über*setzen* ist *über*setzen, traducere navem. Wer nun, zur seefahrt aufgelegt, ein schif bemannen und mit vollem segel an das gestade jenseits führen kann, musz dennoch landen, wo andrer boden ist und andre luft streicht. (Störig, 1963: 111)

This metaphor, in its relevance for translation (i.e. the ship is the text, the navigator is the translator, the passage across the sea or river is the translation process, and the land beyond the two shores are the source and target cultures), can be expanded in the following way:

(1) *Before the departure*
(a) Who sends the ship off on its voyage? Why? Who chooses the cargo and the crew? Who decides about the destination of the journey?
(b) The translator as the responsible navigator must be able to take the ship safely to the other shore
(c) The ship must be solidly built in order to safely take the cargo and/or the passengers to the other shore. This parts of the metaphor relates to conventions of use and to text typologies, to macro- and micro-levels of the text.

(2) *Between the shores, while at sea*
(a) Careful navigation is required. The conditions of the water and the weather have to be taken into account. This relates firstly, to the social embeddedness

of translating, and secondly, to decision-taking concerning the structure of the target text and thus the translation strategies and techniques required.

(b) The value of the cargo has to be judged for the target culture. This relates to the propositional content and the information arrangement in the text as well as to text comprehension.

(3) *Where another wind is blowing.*
(a) How is the text received in the target culture? What effects does it have? Are ship, crew and cargo welcome and accepted in the new culture?

All these questions are relevant for translation, and the answers we find to each of them decide about the translation strategies and techniques to be employed in each individual case.

The huge number of texts that are translated annually throughout the world is evidence that translation is a vital element in fostering intercultural communication.

Future Seminars

The next issue of the journal deals with the topic of 'Multilingualism and monolingualism in Quebec and Catalonia' and the two contributors are John Edwards, St Francis Xavier University, Nova Scotia and Charlotte Hoffmann, University of Salford.

Anyone interested in attending future seminars should contact the Editor, CILS, Department of Languages and European Studies, Aston University, Birmingham B4 7ET, UK (Tel: +44 121 359 3611 ext 4234; e-mail: s.m.wright @aston.ac.uk)

References

Chesterman, A. (1993) Theory in translation theory. *The New Courant* 1, 69–79.

Grass, G. (1984) A tribunal of translators. *Translation* 12, 19.

Macura, V. (1990) Culture as translation. In S. Bassnett and A. Lefevere (eds) *Translation, History and Culture* (pp. 64–70). Pinter: London and New York.

Neubert, A. (1985) *Text and Translation (Übersetzungswissenschaftliche Beiträge 8)*. Leipzig: Enzyklopädie.

Nida, E. (1994) Sociolinguistics as a crucial factor in translating and interpreting (manuscript).

Savory, T.H. (1968) *The Art of Translation*. London: Cape.

Schäffner, C. and Herting, B. (1994) The revolution of the magic lantern: A cross-cultural comparison of translation strategies. In M. Snell-Hornby (1994) (ed.) *Translation Studies: An Interdiscipline* (pp. 27–36). Philadelphia, New York: Benjamins.

Schleiermacher, F. (1838) Über verschiedene Methoden des Übersetzens. *Sämtliche Werke, Abt. 3: Zur Philosophie, Bd. 2*. Berlin.

Snell-Hornby, M. (1988) *Translation Studies: An Integrated Approach*. Philadelphia, New York: Benjamins.

Störig, H.J. (ed) (1963) *Das Problem des Übersetzens*. Darmstadt: Deutsche Buchgemeinschaft.

Venuti, L. (1994) Publishing strategies in translation (manuscript).

Vermeer, H. (1992) Is translation a linguistic or a cultural process? In M. Coulthard (ed.) *Studies in translation/Estudos in tradução, Ilha do Desterro* 28, 37–49.

Weck, G. (1876) *Prinzipien der Übersetzungskunst*. Rawitsch.

TRANSLATION AND THE FORMATION OF CULTURAL IDENTITIES

Lawrence Venuti

Department of English, College of Arts and Sciences, Temple University, Anderson Hall (022–29), Philadelphia, Pennsylvania 19122, USA

Abstract Translation wields enormous power in constructing representations of foreign cultures, while it simultaneously constructs domestic subjects. Translations can have conservative or transgressive effects. Often the translation is erased by suppressing the linguistic and cultural differences of the foreign text, assimilating it to dominant values in the target-language culture, making it recognisable and therefore seemingly untranslated. Foreignising and domesticating are seen as the two main translation strategies. By examining several translation projects from different periods it is shown how translation forms particular cultural identities and maintains them with a relative degree of coherence and homogeneity. The examples fall into the broad category of literary texts. Particular consideration is given to the ethnocentric canon of Japanese fiction in English which reflects a domestic nostalgia for an exotic pre-war Japan; English translations of Aristotle's *Poetics* and their effects on classical scholarship; and the controversies surrounding Jerome's translation of the Old Testament in the early Christian Church. The paper concludes with a consideration of how translation creates possibilities for cultural resistance, innovation, and change.

Introduction

Translation proceeds according to a double bind that gives it the potential to produce far-reaching social effects. As a rule, the translator aims to communicate a foreign text, so that the work of translation is governed by a notion of equivalence that is developing and variable, an equivalence to an interpretation of a foreign form and meaning, usually worked out in the translating process and rarely articulated independently of it. Yet because this interpretation is determined by various domestic factors — most decisively, the translator's knowledge of the foreign language and culture, as well as their relation to domestic cultural values — a translation always communicates a foreign text that is partial and altered, supplemented with features peculiar to the translating language. In fact, the goal of communication can be achieved only when the foreign text is no longer inscrutably foreign, but made comprehensible in a distinctively domestic form.

Translation is thus an inevitable domestication, wherein the foreign text is inscribed with linguistic and cultural values that are intelligible to specific domestic constituencies. This process of inscription operates at every stage in the production, circulation, and reception of the translation. It is initiated by the very choice of a foreign text to translate, always an exclusion of other foreign texts and literatures which answers to particular domestic interests. It continues most forcefully in the development of a translation strategy that rewrites the foreign text in domestic dialects and discourses, always a choice of certain domestic values to the exclusion of others. And it is further complicated by the various forms in which the translation is published, reviewed, read, and taught, producing cultural and political effects that vary with different institutional contexts and social positions.

By far the most consequential of these effects, I want to argue, is the formation of cultural identities. Translation wields enormous power in constructing representations of foreign cultures. The selection of foreign texts and the development of translation strategies can establish peculiarly domestic canons for foreign literatures, canons that conform to domestic aesthetic values and therefore reveal exclusions and admissions, centres and peripheries that deviate from those current in the foreign language. Foreign literatures tend to be dehistoricised by the domestic selection of texts for translation, removed from the foreign literary traditions where they draw their significance; and foreign texts are often rewritten to conform to styles and themes that currently prevail in domestic literatures. These effects may well assume national proportions: translation can create stereotypes for foreign countries that reflect domestic cultural and political values and thereby exclude debates and conflicts that do not appear to serve domestic agendas. Translation is instrumental in shaping domestic attitudes towards foreign countries, attaching esteem or stigma to specific ethnicities, races, and nationalities, able to foster respect for cultural difference or hatred based on ethnocentrism, racism, or patriotism. In the long run, translation figures in geopolitical relations by establishing the cultural grounds of diplomacy, reinforcing alliances, antagonisms, and hegemonies between nations.

Yet since translations are usually designed for specific cultural constituencies, they set in motion a process of identity formation that is double-edged. As translation constructs a domestic representation for a foreign text and culture, it simultaneously constructs a domestic subject, a position of intelligibility that is also an ideological position, shaped by the codes and canons, interests and agendas of certain domestic social groups. Circulating in the church, the state, and the school, a translation can be powerful in maintaining or revising the hierarchy of values in the translating language. A calculated choice of foreign text and translation strategy can change or consolidate literary canons, conceptual paradigms, research methodologies, clinical techniques, and commercial practices in the domestic culture. Whether the effects of a translation prove to be conservative or transgressive depends fundamentally on the discursive strategies developed by the translator, but also on the various factors in their reception, including the page design and cover art of the printed book, the advertising copy, the opinions of reviewers, and the uses made of the translation in cultural and social institutions, how it is read and taught. Such factors mediate the impact of any translation by assisting in the positioning of domestic subjects, equipping them with specific reading practices, affiliating them with specific cultural values and constituencies, reinforcing or crossing institutional limits.

I want to develop these observations by examining several translation projects from different periods, past and present. Each project exhibits in an especially clear way the process of identity formation at work in translation, as well as its diverse effects. The aim is to consider how translation forms particular cultural identities and maintains them with a relative degree of coherence and homogeneity, but also how it creates possibilities for cultural resistance, innovation, and change at any historical moment. For, notwithstanding the fact that translation is summoned to address the linguistic and cultural difference of a foreign text, it can just as effectively foster or suppress heterogeneity in the domestic culture.

The Representation of Foreign Cultures

In 1962 the classical scholar John Jones published a study that challenged the dominant interpretation of Greek tragedy, which, he argued, was not only articulated in academic literary criticism, but inscribed in scholarly editions and translations of Aristotle's *Poetics*. In Jones's view, 'the *Poetics* which we have appropriated to ourselves derives jointly from modern classical scholarship, and from Romanticism' (Jones, 1962: 12). Guided by a Romantic concept of individualism, in which human agency is seen as self-determining, modern scholars have given a psychological cast to Aristotle's concept of tragedy, shifting the emphasis from the action to the hero and the audience's emotional response. This individualistic interpretation, Jones felt, obscures the fact that 'the centre of gravity of Aristotle's terms is situational and not personal', that ancient Greek culture conceived of human subjectivity as socially determinate, 'realised in action and recognised — intelligibly differentiated — through its truth to type' and 'status' (Jones, 1962: 16, 55). Jones's study was favourably reviewed on publication, despite some complaints about his unfamiliar 'jargon' and 'a certain opacity of language', and over the next two decades it gained enormous authority in classical scholarship (Gellie, 1963: 354; Burnett, 1963: 177). By 1977 it had established a 'new orthodoxy' on the question of characterisation in Aristotle's *Poetics* and Greek tragedy, overcoming the long dominance of the hero-centred approach and receiving both assent and further development in the work of leading scholars (Taplin, 1977: 312; Goldhill, 1986: 170–1).

Jones's study proved so effective in causing a disciplinary revision partly because he wrote critiques on the standard translations of Aristotle's treatise. He shrewdly demonstrated that scholarly translators imposed the individualistic interpretation on the Greek text through various lexical choices. From Ingram Bywater's 1909 version he quoted the passage in which Aristotle discusses *hamartia*, the error of judgement made by characters in tragedies. Jones read the English translation symptomatically, locating 'discrepancies' or deviations from the Greek that reveal the work of the translator's ideology, Romantic individualism:

> There are three discrepancies to be noted between Bywater's translation and the Greek original. Where he has 'a good man' the Greek has 'good men'; where he has 'a bad man' the Greek has 'bad men'; and where he renders 'the change in the hero's fortunes' the Greek has 'the change of fortune'. The first and second of his alterations are not quite as trivial as they seem, for they contrive jointly to suggest that Aristotle has in mind a

single dominant figure throughout, when in fact his discourse shifts from plural to singular. These two alterations help pave the way for the third, which is, in the whole range of its implications, momentous. [...] Aristotle's demand that the change of fortune shall be brought about by the *hamartia* of 'the intermediate kind of personage' does not entitle us to style that personage the Tragic Hero; for to call him the hero can only mean that we put him at the centre of our ideal play — as commentator after commentator has alleged that Aristotle does, thrusting the hero on his treatise. (Jones, 1962: 19–20)

Jones was careful to stress that the discrepancies in Bywater's translation are not errors, but calculated choices designed 'to make Aristotle's indisputable meaning plainer than it would otherwise have been' (Jones, 1962: 20). Nonetheless, to make the meaning plain was to make it anachronistic by assimilating the Greek text to a modern cultural concept, 'the now settled habit in which we see action issuing from a solitary focus of consciousness — secret, inward, interesting' (Jones, 1962: 33). The same Romantic inscription is evident in scholarly renderings of the Greek word *mellein*. Jones pointed out that this verb can have several meanings, including 'to be about to do', 'to be on the point of doing', and 'to intend doing'. Both Bywater and Gerald Else (1957) made choices that psychologise Aristotle's concept of tragic action by introducing intentionality and introspection: 'intending to kill', 'intending to betray', 'meditating some deadly injury' (Jones, 1962: 49).

The case of Jones shows that, despite strict canons of accuracy, even academic translations construct distinctly domestic representations of foreign texts and cultures. And these representations, assigned varying degrees of institutional authority, may reproduce or revise dominant conceptual paradigms in academic disciplines. Translations can precipitate a disciplinary revision because the representations they construct are never seamless or perfectly consistent, but often contradictory, assembled from heterogeneous cultural materials, domestic and foreign, past and present. Thus, Jones was able to detect what he called 'discrepancies' in Bywater's translation, discontinuities with the Greek text that signalled the intervention of a modern individualistic ideology.

Yet disciplines also change because competing representations emerge to challenge those in dominance. Although Jones undoubtedly illuminated neglected and distorted aspects of Aristotle's *Poetics* and Greek tragedy, he was himself translating and therefore constructing a domestic representation that was also anachronistic to some extent, even though more compelling than the current academic orthodoxy. As reviewers suggested, Jones's concept of determinate subjectivity reveals an 'existentialist manner of thinking ' that enabled him both to question the individualism of classical scholarship and to develop an interdisciplinary method of reading, not psychological but 'sociological' and 'anthropological' (Bacon, 1963: 56; Burnett, 1963: 176–7; Lucas, 1963: 272). At points, Jones's critique of the orthodox reading clearly resembles the thinking of philosophers like Nietzsche who were important for the emergence of existentialism. Just as *On the Genealogy of the Morals* treats the concept of an autonomous subject as 'the misleading influence of language', wherein '"the doer" is merely a fiction added to the deed', so Jones points to the grammatical category underlying the hero-centred approach to Greek tragedy: 'the status of action must always be adjectival: action qualifies; it tells us things we want to know about the individual promoting it [,...] the state of affairs "inside" him who acts' (Nietzsche, 1967: 45; Jones, 1962: 33). Jones's study was able to establish a new orthodoxy in classical scholarship because it met scholarly standards for textual evidence and critical argument, but also because it reflected the rise of existentialism as a powerful current in post-World War II culture. His critique of the authoritative English translations, along with his own versions of the Greek text, brought about a disciplinary revision by importing cultural values, domestic and foreign, from outside the boundaries of the discipline — notably a concept of determinate subjectivity that was elaborated in German and French philosophers like Heidegger and Sartre and given international currency through translations.

Thus, when an academic translation constructs a domestic representation of a foreign text and culture, this representation can alter the institution where it is housed because disciplinary boundaries are permeable. Although defined by precise qualifications and practices and by a hierarchical arrangement of themes and methodologies, an academic discipline does not reproduce them in an untroubled fashion because it is prone to conceptual infiltrations from other fields and disciplines, both in and out of the academy. And since these boundaries can be crossed, the traffic in cultural values can take diverse forms, not only circulating among academic disciplines, as in the case of Jones, but also moving from one cultural institution to another, as when the academy influences the nature and volume of translations issued by the publishing industry. Here a specific cultural constituency controls the representation of foreign literatures for other constituencies in the domestic culture, privileging certain domestic values to the exclusion of others and establishing a canon of foreign texts that is necessarily partial because it serves certain domestic interests.

A case in point is the translation of modern Japanese fiction into English. As Edward Fowler (1992) demonstrates, American publishers like Grove Press, Alfred Knopf, and New Directions, noted for their concern with literary as well as commercial values, issued many translations of Japanese novels and story collections during the 1950s and 1960s. Yet their choices were very selective, focusing on relatively few writers, mainly Tanizaki Jun'ichiro, Kawabata Yasunari, and Mishima Yukio. By the late 1980s a reviewer who is also a poet and translator could say that 'for the average Western reader, [Kawabata's novel] *Snow Country* is perhaps what we think of as typically "Japanese": elusive, misty, inconclusive' (Kizer, 1988: 80). The same cultural image was assumed by another, more self-conscious reviewer, who, when confronted with an English version of a comic Japanese novel, wondered sceptically: 'Could it be that the novel of delicacy, taciturnity, elusiveness, and languishing melancholy — traits we have come to think of as characteristically Japanese — is less characteristic than we thought?' (Leithauser, 1989: 105). American publishers, Fowler argues, established a canon of Japanese fiction in English that was not only unrepresentative, but based on a well-defined stereotype that has determined reader expectations for roughly 40 years. Moreover, the cultural stereotyping performed by this canon extended beyond English, since English translations of Japanese fiction were routinely translated into other European languages during the same period. In effect, 'the tastes of English-speaking readers have by and large dictated the tastes of the entire Western world with regard to Japanese fiction' (Fowler, 1992: 15–16).

Among the many remarkable things about this canon formation is the fact that the English-speaking tastes in question belonged to a limited group of readers, primarily academic specialists in Japanese literature associated with trade publishers. The translations of Tanizaki, Kawabata, and Mishima were produced by university professors such as Howard Hibbett, Donald Keene, Ivan Morris, and Edward Seidensticker who advised editors on which Japanese texts to publish in English (Fowler, 1992: 12n25). The various interests of these academic translators and their editors — literary, ethnographic, economic — were decisively shaped by an encounter with Japan around the time of the Second World War, and the canon they established constituted a nostalgic image of a lost past. Not only did the translated fiction often refer to traditional Japanese culture, but some novels lamented the disruptive social changes wrought by military conflict and western influence; Japan was represented as 'an exoticised, aestheticised, and quintessentially *foreign* land quite antithetical to its pre-war image of a bellicose and imminently threatening power' (Fowler, 1992: 3, his emphasis).

The nostalgia expressed by the canon was distinctly American, not necessarily shared by Japanese readers. Keene, for example, a critic and translator of considerable authority in English-language culture, disagreed on both literary and political grounds with the lukewarm Japanese reception of Tanizaki's novels. 'Tanizaki seems to have been incapable of writing a boring line', Keene felt, while expressing particular admiration for *The Makioka Sisters*, a novel that was banned by the militaristic government in the early 1940s: 'the leisurely pace of its account of pre-war Japan seems to have exasperated those who insisted on a positive, exhortatory literature suited to the heroic temper of the times' (Keene, 1984: I, 721, 774). Thus, the nostalgic image projected by the canon could carry larger, geopolitical implications: 'the aestheticised realms [in the novels selected for translation] provided exactly the right image of Japan at a time when that country was being transformed, almost overnight in historical terms, from a mortal enemy during the Pacific War to an indispensable ally during the Cold War era' (Fowler, 1992: 6). The English-language canon of Japanese fiction functioned as a domestic cultural support for American diplomatic relations with Japan, which were also designed to contain Soviet expansionism in the east.

This case shows that even when translation projects reflect the interests of a specific cultural constituency — here an elite group of academic specialists and literary publishers — the resulting image of the foreign culture may still achieve national dominance, accepted by many readers in the domestic culture whatever their social position may be. An affiliation between the academy and the publishing industry can be especially effective in moulding a broad consensus, since both possess cultural authority of sufficient power to marginalise non-canonical texts in the domestic culture. The Japanese novels that were not consistent with the post-war academic canon, because they were comic, for example, or represented a more contemporary, westernised Japan — these novels were not translated into English or, if translated, were positioned on the fringes of English-language literature, published by smaller, more specialised publishers (Kodansha International, Charles E. Tuttle) with limited distribution (Fowler, 1992: 14–17). Moreover, the canon did not undergo any significant change during the 1970s and 1980s. The volume of English-language translations suffered a general decline, weakening any effort to widen the range of Japanese novels available in English versions; in the hierarchy of languages translated into English, Japanese ranked sixth after French, German, Russian, Spanish, and Italian (Venuti, 1995: 13; Grannis, 1993: 502). Perhaps more importantly, the institutional programs developed to improve cross-cultural exchange between the United States and Japan continued to be dominated by 'a professional group of university professors and corporate executives (the latter mostly publishers and booksellers) — men whose formative experiences have been shaped by the Second World War' (Fowler, 1992: 25). As a result, the lists of Japanese texts proposed for English translation simply reinforced the established criteria for canonicity, including a special emphasis on the war era and reflecting a 'concern with "high culture" and with the experiences of Japan's intellectual and social elite' (Fowler, 1992: 27).

What this suggests is that translation projects can effect a change in a domestic representation of a foreign culture, not simply when they revise the canons of the most influential cultural constituency, but when another constituency in a different social situation produces and responds to the translations. By the end of the 1980s the academic canon of Japanese literature was being questioned by a new generation of English-language writers and readers. Born after the Pacific war and under the global reach of American hegemony, they were sceptical of 'the down-dragging melancholy of so much Japanese fiction' and more receptive to different forms and themes, including comic narratives that display the deep entrenchment of western cultural influences in Japan (Leithauser, 1989: 110).

Anthologies seem to have played a role in this canon reformation, since, as André Lefevere has shown, 'once a certain degree of early canonisation has been attained' by a foreign literature in translation, 'new anthologies can accept that emerging canon, try to subvert it, or try to enlarge it' (Lefevere, 1992a: 126–7). In 1991, for example, Alfred Birnbaum, an American journalist who was born in 1957 and has lived in Japan since childhood, edited an anthology entitled *Monkey Brain Sushi*. As the sensational title suggests, Birnbaum sought to challenge the academic canon and reach a wider English-language audience with the most recent Japanese fiction. His introduction makes clear that he deliberately avoided the 'staples of the older diet', like Tanizaki, Kawabata, and Mishima, in favour of writers who 'were all born and raised in an Americanised post-war Japan' and whose books are 'what most people really read' (Birnbaum, 1991: 1; for a similar translation project, see Mitsios, 1991). Unlike the older anthologies that established the academic canon — e.g. Keene's Grove Press collection (1956) — Birnbaum's was published by the small American branch of a Tokyo-based press,

Kodansha, and neither the editor nor his three collaborators were affiliated with academic institutions. The early indications are that anthologies like *Monkey Brain Sushi* and Helen Mitsios's *New Japanese Voices* have indeed reformed the canon of Japanese fiction for a popular readership: not only have these books been reprinted in paperback editions, but in their wake several novels by young Japanese writers have been published in English with critical and commercial success.

Perhaps the clearest sign of the change is Banana Yoshimoto's *Kitchen* (1993), which was excerpted in Mitsios's anthology. Yoshimoto was published by one of the presses important for creating the academic canon, Grove, but not on the advice of academic specialists: the editor learned of it through an Italian translation — a change from the period when English was the language through which Japanese fiction was disseminated in European cultures (Harker, 1994: 4). The two pieces in *Kitchen*, a novella and a short story, present Japanese characters who are youthful and extremely westernised, traits that were repeatedly cited as sources of fascination in the reviews. Interestingly, some reviewers assimilated the title piece to aspects of Japanese fiction highlighted by the academic canon. 'Ms Yoshimoto's story', wrote Michiko Kakutani in *The New York Times*, 'turns out not to be a whimsical comedy of manners but an oddly lyrical tale about loss and grief and familial love' (Kakutani, 1993: C15). In a study of the various factors determining the production and reception of *Kitchen*, Jaime Harker attributes its success to the creation of a 'middle-brow' audience for Japanese fiction, an audience that is rather different from the elite academic specialists who formerly selected the texts for translation, even if it still betrays the residual influence of their decades-long dominance. In Harker's view, the appeal of the translation was due to

> a writer who explodes the image of Japanese literature as inscrutable and uninteresting with subject matter which is upbeat, vaguely titillating, and accessibly philosophical; offhand references to American popular culture which create a sense of familiarity for English readers; an accessible yet still 'oriental' translation; and skilful packaging and marketing. The success of *Kitchen*, ultimately, comes from both its effective utilisation, and deformation, of common cultural tropes of 'Japanese-ness'. (Harker, 1994: 1–2)

If the new wave of translated Japanese fiction brings about an enduring canon reformation, it too may harden into a cultural stereotype of Japan — especially if Japanese remains low in the hierarchy of languages translated into English and a narrow range of Japanese texts is made available. Obviously this stereotype will differ from its predecessor in being neither exoticised nor aestheticised, and it will carry rather different geopolitical implications from those that obtained in the post-World War II period. Since the new fiction projects the image of a highly Americanised Japanese culture, at once youthful and energetic, it implicitly answers to current American anxieties about Japan's ascendancy in the global economy, offering an explanation that is reassuringly familiar and not a little self-congratulatory: the image permits Japanese economic power to be seen as an effect of American cultural domination on a later, post-war generation. Thus,

Birnbaum's introduction to his canon-revising anthology informed American readers that, 'trade imbalance notwithstanding, the Japanese have been enthusiastic importers of Western language' (Birnbaum, 1991: 2). The Japanese title of Yoshimoto's novella is in fact a Japanised English word, transliterated as *Kitchen* (Hanson, 1993: 18). The image of contemporary Japanese culture projected by the new fiction may also be traced with a nostalgia for a lost past, although a past that is American, not Japanese, the period from the mid-1940s to the late 1960s, when American hegemony had yet to be decisively challenged at home or abroad.

The Creation of Domestic Subjects

In the foregoing cases, not only do translation projects construct uniquely domestic representations of foreign cultures, but since these projects address specific cultural constituencies, they are simultaneously engaged in the formation of domestic identities. When Jones's existentialist-informed translations of Aristotle displaced the dominant academic reading, they acquired such institutional authority as to become a professional qualification for classical scholars. Specialists in Aristotle and Greek tragedy are expected to demonstrate familiarity with Jones's study in teaching and research publications. Accordingly, Jones rates a mention in introductory surveys of criticism, whether they are devoted to the tragic genre or specific tragedians (e.g. Buxton, 1984). He has also influenced research in such other areas of classical literature as Homeric poetry (Redfield, 1975: 24–6). Similarly, the post-war canon of Japanese fiction in English translation shaped the preferences of both the publishers who invested in elite foreign literature and the readers interested in it. Familiarity with Tanizaki, Kawabata, and Mishima became the mark of a literary taste that was both discriminating and knowledgeable, backed by scholarly credentials.

Of course, the cultural agents who carried out these translation projects did not plan or perhaps even anticipate such domestic effects as the establishment of a professional qualification and the creation of literary taste. They were scholars, translators, and publishers who were more immediately concerned with questions specific to their respective disciplines and practices, questions of academic knowledge, aesthetic value, and commercial success. The history of translation reveals other projects that were designed precisely to form domestic cultural identities by appropriating foreign texts. In these cases, the translations have tended to be highly literary, designed to foster a new literary movement, constructing an authorial subject through an affiliation with a particular literary discourse.

Ezra Pound, for instance, saw translation as a means of cultivating modernist poetic values like linguistic precision. In 1918 he published a 'brief recapitulation and retrospect' of the 'new fashion in poetry' in which he offered the aspiring modernist poet a recipe for self-fashioning (Pound, 1954: 3). 'Translation', he wrote, is 'good training, if you find that your original matter "wobbles" when you try to rewrite it. The meaning of the poem to be translated can not "wobble"' (Pound, 1954: 7). Modernist poets like Pound translated foreign texts that supported modernist poetic language: 'In the art of Daniel and Cavalcanti', he remarked, 'I have seen that precision which I miss in the Victorians' (Pound, 1954: 11). Pound fashioned himself as a modernist poet-translator partly by competing against Victorian translators of the poems he valued, imitating yet exceeding them in specific translation choices. He introduced his translation of Guido Cavalcanti's poetry by admitting that 'in the matter of these translations and of my knowledge of Tuscan poetry, Rossetti is my father and mother, but no man can see everything at once' (Anderson, 1983: 14).

The case of Pound suggests not merely that translation can be instrumental in the construction of an authorial identity, but also that this construction is at once discursive and psychological, worked out in writing practices open to psycho-analytic interpretation. Pound's translations staged an oedipal rivalry in which he challenged Rossetti's canonical status by translating poetry the Victorian poet had translated, Cavalcanti's idealised representations of women (Venuti, 1995: 197). In the process Pound defined himself both as modernist and as male. He felt that his translations supplied what had 'escaped' Rossetti, namely 'a robustezza, a masculinity' (Anderson, 1983: 243). Which is to say that, in his own view, Pound bettered his poetic father in capturing the female image presented by a foreign poetry.

Because translation can contribute to the invention of domestic literary discourses, it has inevitably been enlisted in ambitious cultural projects, notably the development of a domestic language and literature. And such projects have always resulted in the formation of cultural identities aligned with specific social groups, with classes and nations. During the 18th and 19th centuries German translation was theorised and practised as a means of developing a German-language literature. In 1813 the philosopher Friedrich Schleiermacher pointed out to his scholarly German audience that 'much of what is beautiful and powerful in our language has in part either developed by way of translation or been drawn out by translation' (Lefevere, 1992b: 165). Schleiermacher put translation in the service of a bourgeois cultural elite, a largely professional readership which preferred a highly refined German literature grounded in classical texts. Yet he and contemporaries like Goethe and the Schlegel brothers viewed these minority values as defining a national German culture to the exclusion of various popular genres and texts — mainly the sentimental realism, Gothic tales, chivalric romances, and didactic biographies preferred by the largest segment of German-language readers (Venuti, 1995: 105–10).

In 1827 Goethe noted that 'flagging national literatures are revived by the foreign', and he then proceeded to describe the specular mechanism by which a domestic subject is formed in translation:

> In the end every literature grows bored if it is not refreshed by foreign participation. What scholar does not delight in the wonders wrought by mirroring and reflection? And what mirroring means in the moral sphere has been experienced by everyone, perhaps unconsciously; and, if one stops to consider, one will realise how much of his own formation throughout life he owes to it. (Berman, 1992: 65)

Translation forms domestic subjects by enabling a process of 'mirroring' or self-recognition: the foreign text becomes intelligible when the reader recognises him- or herself in the translation by identifying the domestic values that motivated the selection of that particular foreign text, and that are inscribed in it through a particular discursive strategy. The self-recognition is a recognition of the domestic cultural norms and resources that constitute the self, that define it *narcissim* as a domestic subject. The process is basically narcissistic: the reader identifies with an ideal projected by the translation, usually values that have achieved authority in the domestic culture and dominate those of other cultural constitu-encies. Sometimes, however, the values may be currently marginal yet ascendant, mobilised in a challenge to the dominant. At Goethe's moment, when the Napoleonic wars threatened to extend French domination into Prussia, a compelling ideal was a nationalist concept of a distinctively German literary culture, underwritten by the translation of canonical foreign texts but still to be realised. As Antoine Berman has remarked of Goethe's thinking, 'foreign literatures become the mediators in the internal conflicts of national literatures and offer them an image of themselves they could not otherwise have', but which, we may add, they nonetheless desire (Berman, 1992: 65). Hence, the reader's self-recognition is also a misrecognition: a domestic inscription is taken for the foreign text, dominant domestic values for the reader's own, and the values of one constituency for those of all others in the domestic culture. Goethe's mention of 'scholar' is a reminder that the subject constructed by this nationalist agenda for translation entails an affiliation with a specific social group, here a minority with sufficient cultural authority to set itself up as the arbiter of a national literature.

Translations thus position readers in domestic intelligibilities that are also ideological positions, ensembles of values, beliefs, and representations that further the interests of certain social groups over others. In cases where translations are housed in institutions like the church, the state, or the school, the identity-forming process enacted by a translated text potentially affects social reproduction by providing a sense of what is true, good, and possible (see Therborn, 1980). Translations may maintain existing social relations by investing domestic subjects with the ideological qualification to assume a role or perform a function in an institution. But they may also bring about social change by revising such qualifications and thereby modifying institutional roles or func-tions. The social impact of a translation depends on its discursive strategies and on its reception, both of which figure in the identity-forming process.

Consider the controversies surrounding the translation of the Bible in the early Christian Church. The Septuagint, the Greek version of the Old Testament prepared by Hellenistic Jews in the third century B.C., still commanded enormous authority some six centuries later: it was the ground of all theological and exegetical speculation, and it displaced the Hebrew text as the source of the Latin translations that were widely used by Christian congregations in the late Roman Empire. Augustine, bishop of Hippo, feared Jerome's project of translat-ing the Old Testament directly from the Hebrew because it threatened the ideological consistency and institutional stability of the Church. In a letter to Jerome written in 403, Augustine explained that 'many problems would arise if your translation began to be read regularly in many churches, because the Latin churches would be out of step with the Greek ones' (White, 1990: 92). Augustine then described an incident which demonstrated that early Christian identity was deeply rooted in the Septuagint and in the Latin translations made from it; to introduce Jerome's translation from the Hebrew would throw this identity into crisis and ultimately play havoc with Church organisation by alienating believers:

> when one of our fellow bishops arranged for your translation to be read in a church in his diocese, they came across a word in your version of the prophet Jonah which you had rendered very differently from the transla-tion with which they were familiar and which, having been read by so many generations, was ingrained in their memories. A great uproar ensued in the congregation, especially among the Greeks who criticised the text and passionately denounced it as wrong, and the bishop (the incident took place in the city of Oea) was compelled to ask the Jews to give evidence. Whether out of ignorance or spite, they replied that this word did occur in the Hebrew manuscripts in exactly the same form as in the Greek and Latin versions. In short, the man was forced to correct the passage in your version as if it were inaccurate since he did not want this crisis to leave him without a congregation. This makes us suspect that you, too, can be mistaken occasionally. (White, 1990: 92–3)

The Septuagint-based Latin translation used at Oea formed Christian identities by sustaining a self-recognition that defined orthodox belief: members of the congregation recognised themselves as Christians on the basis of an institution-ally validated translation that was 'familiar' and 'ingrained in their memories'. The furor caused by Jerome's version from the Hebrew shows that the continued existence of the institution requires a relatively stable process of identity formation enacted not simply by a particular translation, but by the repeated use of it — 'read by so many generations'. It is also clear that the institution ensures the stability of the identity-forming process by erecting a criterion for translation accuracy: members of the congregation, especially Greeks, judged a Latin version of the Old Testament 'correct' when they found its renderings consistent with the authoritative Greek version, the Septuagint.

Yet a cultural practice like translation can also precipitate social change because neither subjects nor institutions can ever be completely coherent or sealed off from the diverse ideologies that circulate in the domestic culture. Identity is never irrevocably fixed but rather relational, the nodal point for a multiplicity of practices and institutions whose sheer heterogeneity creates the possibility for change (Laclau & Mouffe, 1985: 105–14). Jerome insisted on a return to the Hebrew text partly because his cultural identity was Latin as well as Christian and distinguished by a highly refined literary taste: educated in Rome, 'he was part of a culture in which sensitivity to a foreign language was an integral element', so that 'he was capable of appreciating the aesthetic merits of works in a language not his own', like the Hebrew Bible (Kamesar, 1993: 43, 48–9). The polylingualism of Latin literary culture combined with Christian belief to motivate Jerome's study of Hebrew, eventually enabling his discovery that the authoritative Greek translations and editions were deficient: his Latin versions of them, as he explained to Augustine, contained typographical indicators for passages where 'the Septuagint expands on the Hebrew text' or 'something has been added by Origen from the edition of Theodotion' (White, 1990: 133). Jerome's complicated cultural make-up led him to question the Septuagint: whereas its authority among the Church Fathers rested on a belief in its divine inspiration as well as the Apostles' approval of its use, Jerome's concern for textual integrity and doctrinal authenticity judged it inadequate, flawed by omissions and expansions that reflected the values of its pagan patron and corrupted by variants that accumulated in successive editions (Kamesar, 1993: 59–69).

Jerome's translation did finally displace the Septuagint, becoming the standard Latin version of the Bible throughout the medieval period and beyond while exerting 'an incalculable influence not only on the piety but on the languages and literatures of western Europe' (Kelly, 1975: 162). This success was due in large part to Jerome's discursive strategies and to the prefaces and letters in which he defended his version. His translation discourse reveals his cultural diversity. On the one hand, he Latinised characteristic features of the Hebrew text by revising simple paratactic constructions into complex suspended periods and by replacing the formulaic repetition of words and phrases with elegant variations (Sparks, 1970: 524–6). On the other hand, he Christianised Judaic themes by rewriting 'a large number of passages in such a way as to give them a much more pointedly Messianic or otherwise Christian implication than the Hebrew permitted' (Kelly, 1975: 162). In adopting such discursive strategies, Jerome's translation appealed to Christians who, like him, were schooled in Latin literary culture.

In defending his translation, furthermore, he anticipated the objections of such Church officials as Augustine, who feared that a return to the Hebrew text would weaken institutional stability. Although extremely critical of the Septuagint, Jerome shrewdly represented his Latin version not as a replacement, but as a supplement, which, like other Latin versions, would aid in the interpretation of the authoritative Greek translation and 'protect Christians from Jewish ridicule and accusations that they were ignorant of the true Scriptures' (Kamesar, 1993: 59). Jerome's version was thus presented as an institutional support, assisting in theological and exegetical speculation and in debates with the members of a rival religious institution — the synagogue — who cast doubt on the cultural authority of Christianity.

The controversies in the early Christian Church make clear that translations can alter the functioning of any social institution because translating, by definition, involves the domestic assimilation of a foreign text. This means that the work of translation must inescapably rely on cultural norms and resources that differ fundamentally from those circulating in the domestic culture. Thus, as Augustine's letter reported, the bishop at Oea was forced to resort to Jewish informants to assess the correctness of Jerome's version from the Hebrew text, even though the criterion of accuracy (viz. fidelity to the Septuagint) was formulated and applied within the Christian Church. By the same token, Jerome's departures from the Septuagint occasionally followed other, more literal Greek versions of the Old Testament made by Jews and used in synagogues (White, 1990: 137). Since the task of translation is to make a foreign text intelligible in domestic terms, the institutions where translations are used become vulnerable to infiltrations from different and even incompatible cultural materials that may controvert authoritative texts and revise prevailing criteria for translation accuracy. Perhaps the domestic identities formed by translation can avoid the dislocations of the foreign only when institutions regulate translation practices so restrictively as to efface and hence defuse the linguistic and cultural differences of foreign texts.

An Ethics of Translation

If translation has such far-reaching social effects, if in forming cultural identities it contributes to social reproduction and change, it seems important to evaluate these effects, to ask whether they are good or bad, or in other words whether the resulting identities are ethical. Here Berman's concept of a translation ethics is useful. For Berman, bad translation is ethnocentric: 'generally under the guise of transmissibility, [it] carries out a systematic negation of the strangeness of the foreign work' (Berman, 1992: 5). Good translation aims to limit this ethnocentric negation by staging 'an opening, a dialogue, a cross-breeding, a decentering' and thereby forcing the domestic language and culture to register the foreignness of the foreign text (Berman, 1992: 4).

A translation ethics, then, cannot be restricted to a notion of fidelity. Not only does a translation constitute an interpretation of the foreign text, varying with different cultural situations at different historical moments, but canons of accuracy are articulated and applied in the domestic culture and therefore are basically ethnocentric. The ethical values governed by such canons are generally professional or institutional, established by academic specialists, publishers, and reviewers and assimilated by translators. A translation ethics, furthermore, cannot assume that translation can ever rid itself of its fundamental domestication, its basic task of rewriting the foreign text in domestic terms. The problem is rather how to redirect the ethnocentric movement of translation so as to decentre the domestic cultural terms that a translation project must inescapably utilise.

In the projects we have examined, the identity-forming process was repeatedly grounded in domestic ideologies and institutions. This suggests that they were all engaged in an ethnocentric reduction of possibilities, excluding not only possible representations of foreign cultures, but also possible constructions of domestic subjects. Yet distinctions can be drawn among the projects. The English-language canon of Japanese fiction, for example, was clearly ethnocentric in Berman's bad sense: although it did indeed represent the Japanese texts as foreign, this representation was distinctively American and academic, reflecting a domestic nostalgia for an exotic pre-war Japan, and it marginalised texts that did not exhibit the privileged concept of foreignness. A nonethnocentric translation project would make available both the exotic and the Americanised (among other excluded forms and themes), inevitably domesticating the texts to some extent, but at the same time representing the diversity of the Japanese narrative tradition by restoring those segments of it that were formerly neglected.

To limit the ethnocentric movement inherent in translation, a project must take into account the interests of more than just those of a cultural constituency that occupies a dominant position in the domestic culture. A translation project must consider the culture where the foreign text originated and address various domestic constituencies. Jones's translations of Aristotle truly decentred the reigning academic versions because his project was open to foreign cultural values that were not located in the English-language academy: the features of the archaic Greek text that were repressed by the modern Anglo-American ideology of individualism became visible from the vantage point of the modern Continental philosophy of existentialism, disseminated in philosophical treatises and literary texts. A nonethnocentric translation project thus alters the reproduction of dominant domestic ideologies and institutions that misrepresent foreign cultures and marginalise other domestic constituencies.

Yet since such a project has the potential to establish a new orthodoxy, it too may eventually come to take on an ethnocentric significance and therefore be subject to displacement by a later nonethnocentric project designed to rediscover a foreign text for a different constituency. William Tyndale's 1525 English version of the New Testament challenged the authority that Jerome's Latin version had acquired in the Catholic Church, and the challenge was instrumental in forming a different religious identity, the English Protestant. Sir Thomas More was quick to perceive the ideological decentering effected by Tyndale's own return to the Greek text: Tyndale, in More's view, 'changed the word church [*ecclesia* in the Greek] into this word congregation, because he would bring it in question which were the church and set forth Luther's heresy that the church which we should believe and obey, is not the common known body of all Christian realms remaining in the faith of Christ' (Lefevere, 1992b: 71).

Nonethnocentric translation reforms cultural identities that occupy dominant positions in the domestic culture, yet in many cases this reformation subsequently issues into another dominance and another ethnocentrism. A translation practice that is rigorously nonethnocentric would seem to be highly subversive of domestic ideologies and institutions. It, too, would form a cultural identity, but one that is simultaneously critical and contingent, constantly assessing the relations between a domestic culture and its foreign others and developing translation projects solely on the basis of changing assessments. Such projects risk unintelligibility, by decentering domestic ideologies too far, and cultural marginality, by destabilising the workings of domestic institutions. Yet since nonethnocentric translation promises a greater openness to cultural differences, whether they are located abroad or at home, they may well be worth the risks.

Acknowledgements

My work on this article benefited from conversations with my colleague Daniel Tompkins, professor of Classics at Temple University.

References

Anderson, D. (ed.) (1983) *Pounds's Cavalcanti: An Edition of the Translations, Notes, and Essays*. Princeton: Princeton University Press.

Bacon, H. (1963) Review of Jones (1962). *The Classical World* 57, 56.

Berman, A. (1992) *The Experience of the Foreign: Culture and Translation in Romantic Germany*. (Trans. S. Heyvaert.) Albany: State University of New York Press.

Birnbaum, A. (ed.) (1991) *Monkey Brain Sushi: New Tastes in Japanese Fiction*. Tokyo and New York: Kodansha International.

Burnett, A.P. (1963) Review of Jones (1962). *Classical Philology* 58, 176–8.

Buxton, R.G.A. (1984) *Sophocles. New Surveys in the Classics* 16. Oxford: Clarendon Press.

Bywater, I. (ed. and trans.) (1909) *Aristotle on the Art of Poetry*. Oxford: Clarendon Press.

Else, G. (ed. and trans.) (1957) *Aristotle's Poetics: The Argument*. Cambridge, MA: Harvard University Press.

Fowler, E. (1992) Rendering words, traversing cultures: On the art and politics of translating modern Japanese fiction. *Journal of Japanese Studies* 18, 1–44.

Gellie, G.H. (1963) Review of Jones (1962). *Journal of the Australasian Language and Literature Association* 20, 353–4.

Goldhill, S. (1986) *Reading Greek Tragedy*. Cambridge and New York: Cambridge University Press.

Grannis, C. (1993) Book title output and average prices: 1992 preliminary figures and U.S. book exports and imports, 1990–1991. In C. Barr (ed.) *The Bowker Annual Library and Book Trade Almanac*. New Providence, New Jersey: Bowker.

Hanson, E. (1993) Hold the Tofu. *The New York Times Book Review*, 17 January, p. 18.

Harker, J. (1994) You can't sell culture: Kitchen and middlebrow translation strategies. Unpublished manuscript.

Jones, J. (1962) *On Aristotle and Greek Tragedy*. London: Chatto and Windus.

Kakutani, M. (1993) Very Japanese, very American and very popular. *The New York Times*, 12 January, p. C15.

Kamesar, A. (1993) *Jerome, Greek Scholarship, and the Hebrew Bible: A Study of the Quaestiones Hebraicae in Genesim*. Oxford: Clarendon Press.

Keene, D. (ed.) (1956) *Modern Japanese Literature: An Anthology*. New York: Grove Press.

— (1984) *Dawn to the West: Japanese Literature of the Modern Era*. New York: Holt, Rinehart, and Winston.

Kelly, J.N.D. (1975) *Jerome: His Life, Writings, and Controversies*. New York: Harper and Row.

Kizer, Carolyn. (1988) Donald Keene and Japanese fiction, Part II. *Delos* 1 (3), 73–94.

Laclau, E. and Mouffe, C. (1985) *Hegemony and Socialist Strategy: Toward a Radical Democratic Politics* (trans. Winston Moore and Paul Cammack). London: Verso.

Lefevere, A. (1992a) *Translation, Rewriting, and the Manipulation of Literary Fame*. London and New York: Routledge.

— (1992b) *Translation/History/Culture: A Sourcebook*. London and New York: Routledge.

Leithauser, B. (1989) An ear for the unspoken. *The New Yorker*, 6 March, pp. 105–111.

Lucas, D.W. (1963) Review of Jones (1962). *The Classical Review* 13, 270–2.

Mitsios, H. (ed.) (1991) *New Japanese Voices: The Best Contemporary Fiction from Japan*. New York: Atlantic Monthly Press.

Nietzsche, F. (1967) *On the Genealogy of Morals* (trans. Walter Kaufmann and R.J. Hollingdale). New York: Random House.

Pound, E. (1954) *Literary Essays* (ed. T.S. Eliot). New York: New Directions.

Redfield, J.M. (1975) *Nature and Culture in the Iliad: The Tragedy of Hector*. Chicago: University of Chicago Press.

Sparks, H.F.D. (1970) Jerome as Biblical Scholar. In P. Ackroyd and C.F. Evans (eds) *The Cambridge History of the Bible* Vol. 1. Cambridge: Cambridge University Press.

Taplin, O. (1977) *The Stagecraft of Aeschylus: The Dramatic Use of Exits and Entrances in Greek Tragedy*. Oxford: Clarendon Press.

Therborn, G. (1980) *The Ideology of Power and the Power of Ideology*. London: Verso.

Venuti, L. (1995) *The Translator's Invisibility: A History of Translation*. London and New York: Routledge.

White, C. (ed. and trans.) (1990) *The Correspondence between Jerome and Augustine of Hippo*. Lewiston, New York: Edwin Mellen Press.

PRELIMINARY REMARKS TO THE DEBATE

Lawrence Venuti

Department of English, College of Arts and Sciences, Temple University, Anderson Hall (022–29), Philadelphia, Pennsylvania 19122, USA

The paper I circulated for the seminar is part of a book-length project that I am tentatively calling *The Scandal of Translation*. This project takes as its point of departure the misunderstanding, suspicion, and neglect that continue to greet the practice of translation, especially in the United States and the United Kingdom. In the major English-speaking countries, not only does the volume of translations published remain low: 2 or 3% of the total annual output (roughly 1200 books), but translation is relatively underfunded by government and private agencies, unfavourably defined by copyright law, and virtually ignored by reviewers and readers. An important reason for this marginality, I want to argue, is that translation scandalises values that have long dominated Anglo-American culture. And like every scandal it calls forth various policing functions designed to enforce the values in question.

Translation is, first, an offence against the prevailing concept of authorship. Whereas authorship is defined as originality, self-expression in a unique text, translation is derivative, neither self-expression nor unique: it imitates another text. Given the reigning concept of authorship, translation provokes the fear of inauthenticity, distortion, contamination. Yet in so far as the translator must focus on the linguistic and cultural constituents of the foreign text, translation may also provoke the fear that the foreign author is not original, but derivative, fundamentally dependent on pre-existing materials. It is partly to quell these fears that translation practices in Anglo-American culture have routinely aimed for their own concealment, at least since the 17th century. In practice, the fact of translation is erased by suppressing the linguistic and cultural differences of the foreign text, assimilating it to dominant values in the target-language culture, making it recognisable and therefore seemingly untranslated. With this domestication the translated text passes for the original, an expression of the foreign author's intention.

Translation is, secondly, an offence against a still prevailing concept of scholarship that rests on the assumption of original authorship. Whereas this scholarship seeks to ascertain the authorial intention that constitutes originality, translation not only deviates from that intention, but substitutes others: it addresses a different audience in a different language. Instead of enabling a true understanding of the foreign text, then, translation provokes the fear of error, amateurism, opportunism. And in so far as the translator focuses on the linguistic and cultural constituents of the foreign text, translation provokes the fear that authorial intention cannot possibly control their meaning and social functioning. Under the burden of these fears, translation has long been marginalised in the study of literature, even in our current situation, where the influx of poststructuralist thinking has decisively questioned author-oriented literary theory and criticism. Whether humanist or poststructuralist, contemporary scholarship tends to assume that translation does not offer a true understanding of the foreign text, or a valuable contribution to the knowledge of literature, domestic or foreign. The effects of this assumption are evident in the hiring, tenure, and promotion practices of academic institutions, as well as in academic publishing. Translation is rarely considered a form of scholarship, it does not currently constitute a qualification for an academic appointment, and translated texts are rarely made the object of research by literary scholars. The fact of translation tends to be ignored even by scholars who must rely on translated texts in their research and teaching.

My project is to explore the continuing scandal of translation in a series of theoretical essays grounded in detailed examinations of actual translation projects, past and present. The aim is to challenge the currently unfavourable situation in which translated texts are produced and used by submitting translation to a thoroughgoing scrutiny and redefinition. The chapters will focus on the relations between translation and cultural categories or practices that have restricted, marginalised, or repressed it: authorship, scholarship, copyright, cultural identity, pedagogy, publishing, adaptation.

My paper for the seminar is intended to suggest that translation is regarded with suspicion partly because it produces far-reaching social effects, including the formation of cultural identities. To develop these theoretical observations, I examine several translation projects which all fall into the broad category of literary translation — philosophical and religious texts, novels, poetry. It may seem, then, that the identity-forming power of translation is most active or most apparent with texts that are designed to do more than communicate, that employ different discursive forms and registers to produce literary effects and thus exceed the communication of a fixed meaning in order to proliferate meanings.

This appearance, however, is misleading: the identity-forming power of translation is just as active and evident with the varieties of technical translation — commercial, legal, scientific, diplomatic — which do indeed aim to communicate a fixed meaning so as to produce predictable social effects. Perhaps the most obvious point here is that technical translations — legal textbooks, say, or instruction manuals — qualify social agents to perform various tasks and functions, professionals as well as consumers, enabling them to achieve and maintain levels of expertise or simply to use a product manufactured in a foreign country. Advertising in particular offers a productive area to study the role played by translation in forming cultural identities, since, as Roland Barthes (1972) has shown, ads enact a semiotic process that in effect mythologises products, investing them with a charismatic significance for the consumer. When these products are foreign, the significance must be domestic, but its reverberations will be intercultural: a translated ad can simultaneously create or revise a stereotype for a foreign culture while appealing to a specific domestic constituency, a specific segment of the domestic market.

Nor should the identity-forming power of translation be seen as applying strictly to print media, whether literary or technical. Dubbing, for example, illustrates quite clearly that the very medium of a translation can sharply distinguish between audiences for foreign film and television. When these media use dubbed translations, they stand to reach larger, popular audiences, whereas translations in the form of subtitles limit their appeal to a smaller, elite audience. In a European country like Italy, Hollywood film and television programmes are generally dubbed, to make them fit for mass consumption; in the United States, Italian films, whether they are art works full of formal experiments or movies in popular genres, tend to be subtitled, shown in repertory theatres and university film courses, appealing to an educated cultural elite.

In the final section of my paper, I take up the issue of a translation ethics by acknowledging that a translator confronts competing ethical imperatives, both toward the foreign text and culture and toward the domestic cultural constituency for which the translation is made. My view is that the translator must be ready to be disloyal to that constituency — contrary to the notion of 'loyalty' developed by Skopostheorists like Nord (1991) — must maintain a constantly critical attitude toward the domestic cultural norms which govern the translation, and which the translation in turn underwrites through the formation of domestic subjects, subject to those norms. This is an ethics of change in which the translator calls attention to what domestic norms enable and limit, admit and exclude, in their encounter with foreign texts and cultures. From this viewpoint, translators can be described, following Anthony Pym, as 'intercultural' subjects, members of a community that straddles cultures and therefore exists potentially in a critical distance from both. As Pym puts it, 'none of us can wholly identify with the people for whom we teach or produce translations' (Pym, 1993: 63). Translation, practised in this nonethnocentric way, is a scandal to ethnocentrism.

But this ethics will not be easy to follow for translators today. To conclude these preliminary remarks, I want to consider an ethical quandary raised by a specific case: the canon of modern Japanese fiction in English. In my paper I argued that this canon was ethnocentric: although it did indeed represent the Japanese texts as foreign, this representation was distinctively American and academic, reflecting a domestic nostalgia for an exotic pre-war Japan, and it marginalised texts that did not exhibit the privileged concept of foreignness. A nonethnocentric translation project would make available both the exotic and the Americanised (among other excluded forms and themes), inevitably domesticating the texts to some extent, but at the same time representing the diversity of the Japanese narrative tradition by restoring those segments of it that were formerly neglected. The question is whether recent translations of Japanese fiction, particularly the novels of Banana Yoshimoto, constitute such a restoration. Masao Miyoshi has judged Yoshimoto's fiction to be a naively written celebration of Americanised Japan, unlike the work of some other Japanese women novelists who are 'critically alert and historically intelligent' (Miyoshi, 1991: 212, 236). Tanizaki's novels, moreover, offer a compelling contrast: Miyoshi writes of *The Makioka Sisters* that 'if the work's apparent lack of interest in the war is a mark of the author's resistance' against Japanese militarism, then 'its indifference to the post-war years may also point to a criticism of the Occupation-imposed reforms' (Miyoshi, 1991: 114). An ethical move, then,

would be to translate Tanizaki instead of Yoshimoto, in contrast to what I —
following Edward Fowler's criticism — have suggested.

This case indicates the need for a more sophisticated concept of the translator's
deviation from domestic cultural norms. What distinguishes Miyoshi's position
from Fowler's is that Miyoshi is rather single-mindedly searching out texts that
are critical of American political and economic hegemony in world affairs,
whereas Fowler is discriminating between specific values within American
culture. While both lines of thinking are important today for any truly ethical
translation, Fowler's implicitly realises that domestic canons for foreign literatures are always already in place when a translation project is developed, and
that therefore a translation ethics must take these canons into account. Put
another way, any agenda of cultural resistance for translation must take
specifically cultural forms, must choose foreign texts and translation methods
that deviate from the canonical or dominant ones. And this a writer like
Yoshimoto definitely does — especially in Megan Backus' English version of
Kitchen.

This version is highly readable, but it is also foreignising in its translation
strategy. Instead of cultivating a seamless fluency that invisibly inscribes
American values in the text, Backus develops an extremely heterogeneous
language that undoubtedly communicates the Americanisation of Japan, but
simultaneously foregrounds the differences between American and Japanese
culture for an English-language reader. The translation generally adheres to the
standard dialect of current English usage but is mixed with other dialects and
discourses. There is a rich strain of colloquialism, mostly American, both in the
lexicon and the syntax: 'cut the crap', 'home-ec' (for Home Economics), 'I'm kind
of in a hurry', 'I perked up', 'I would sort of tortuously make my way', 'night
owl', 'okay', 'slipped through the cracks', 'smart ass', 'three sheets to the wind',
'woozy' (Yoshimoto, 1993: 4, 6, 19, 29, 42, 47, 63, 70, 92, 103). There is also a
recurrent, slightly archaic formality used in passages that express the fey
romanticism to which the narrator, Mikage, is inclined. 'I'm dead worn out, in a
reverie', she says at the opening, combining the poetical archaism 'reverie' with
the colloquialism 'dead worn out' (Yoshimoto, 1993: 4). Similarly, when she first
meets Yuichi, beginning the relationship that drives the narrative, he sends her
language shifting through registers and references, from high-tech slang to
Hollywood love talk to mystical theology:

> His smile was so bright as he stood in my doorway that I zoomed in for a
> close-up on his pupils. I couldn't take my eyes off him. I think I heard a
> spirit call my name. (Yoshimoto, 1993: 6)

There are, moreover, many italicised Japanese words scattered throughout the
text, mostly for food — 'katsudon', 'ramen', 'soba', 'udon', 'wasabi' — but
including other aspects of Japanese culture, like clothing ('obi') and furnishings
('tatami mat') (Yoshimoto, 1993: 40, 61, 78, 83, 89, 98, 100).

The heterogeneity of Backus' translation discourse indicates that Yoshimoto's
characters are Americanised Japanese. The very language of the translation thus
makes the same point that is made in the Japanese text by the many allusions to

American popular culture, to comic strips (Linus), television programmes (*Bewitched*), amusement parks (Disneyland), restaurant chains (Denny's) and so forth (Yoshimoto, 1993: 5, 31, 90, 96). But since the discourse contains so many deviations from the standard dialect, the translation offers a truly delirious experience to an English-language reader, who is constantly made aware that the text is a translation because the discursive effects work only in English. The first ethical move in the case of *Kitchen* is the decision to translate a work of Japanese fiction that runs counter to the post-World War II canon of this genre in English. But the second is to develop a translation discourse that is foreignising in its deviation from dominant linguistic norms, that brings the awareness that the translation is only a translation, imprinted with domestic intelligibilities and interests, and therefore not to be confused with the foreign text.

Miyoshi does not consider these effects because his approach to Yoshimoto's fiction focuses on the Japanese text and its Japanese reception. The Americanised Japan represented in this fiction can only have a different cultural and political significance for American readers who experience Backus' foreignising translation. The limitations of neglecting the issue of translation become most apparent when Miyoshi quotes several passages from *Kitchen* to illustrate his criticism that 'there is no style, no poise, no imagery' (Miyoshi, 1991: 236). He needs to *translate* the Japanese text to make his point, but the difference created by the shift to English does not exist for him. When his translation of a passage is juxtaposed to Backus', the foreignising impulse in her writing emerges quite clearly:

> I placed the bedding in a quiet well-lit kitchen, drawing silently soft sleepiness that comes with saturated sadness not relieved by tears. I fell asleep wrapped in a blanket like Linus [of *Peanuts*]. (Miyoshi, 1991: 236)

> Steeped in a sadness so great I could barely cry, shuffling softly in gentle drowsiness, I pulled my futon into the deathly silent, gleaming kitchen. Wrapped in a blanket, like Linus, I slept. (Yoshimoto, 1993: 4–5)

Backus' version typically opens with the sort of romantic poeticism that characterises Mikage (the subtly metaphorical 'steeped in sadness'), communicated through a suspended syntactical construction that is fluent but formal, even faintly archaic, in its complexity. The lexicon begins to change noticeably with the translator's retention of the Japanese word 'futon', and then again with the American cultural reference ('Linus'). Moreover, the pop familiarity of this reference is somewhat defamiliarised by its placement in a construction that resembles the more formal syntax used in the first sentence. Compared to the heterogeneity of Backus' version, Miyoshi's is domesticating, assimilating the Japanese text to the standard dialect of English, so familiar as to be transparent or seemingly untranslated — even in his eyes. The features of Yoshimoto's Japanese that provokes his criticism are transformed in English, but it is only Backus' English that invites the critical reflection Miyoshi values. The linguistic and cultural differences introduced by any translation can permit a foreign text that seems aesthetically inferior and politically reactionary at home to carry opposite valences abroad.

It is at this point, finally, that the issue of audience assumes importance.

Translations of Yoshimoto's fiction are different, or deviant from reigning canons, because these translations were not developed by or designed for the American cultural elite which maintains the canons. On the contrary, her success in translation is a result of her appeal to a wider, middle-brow readership, youthful and educated, although not necessarily academic. Miyoshi is certainly right to question the Americanised themes in Yoshimoto's fiction, to view them as evidence of the cultural imperialism that the United States has conducted since the Second World War. But he seeks a more sophisticated, modernist form of narrative that in English-language culture appeals to a relatively narrow audience. In suggesting that Yoshimoto is not worth translating, he would prevent a larger American constituency from evaluating the impact of American culture abroad. My conclusion, then, is that translating Yoshimoto at the present moment is an ethical move for an English-language translator to make.

References

Barthes, R. (1972) *Mythologies* (Trans. Annette Lavers) New York: Hill and Wang.
Miyoshi, M. (1991) *Off Center: Power and Culture Relations between Japan and the United States*. Cambridge, MA: Harvard University Press.
Nord, C. (1991) Scopos, loyalty, and translational conventions. *Target* 3 (1), 91–109.
Pym, A. (1993) Why translation conventions should be intercultural rather than culture-specific: An alternative basic-link model. *Paralleles* 15, 60–8.

DEBATE

The Concept of Ethnocentricity

Douglas Robinson (University of Mississipi): I would like to start off the debate by taking up the concept of ethnocentricity you discussed at the end of your paper. I wanted to raise two or three examples which I think all fit into this question about ethnocentricity. When you were talking about the translator leaving the Japanese words in, what occurred to me was the number of novels about Japan which have been written in the post-war era which contain a lot of Japanese. These novels seem to reflect that canon you were talking about, the mystical conception of Japan — for example, James Clavell's *Shogun*. These novels are politically very astute and tend to take a kind of foreignising approach in the sense that the heroes tend to be Americans who have been very strongly assimilated into Japanese culture through martial arts, linguistic training and various things. So, there's a tendency among publishers to be interested in American cultural imperialism in Japan. *Kitchen* turns that around and tends to be interested in Japanese economic imperialism in the USA. Another one is Tom Clancy. And all these people are using this device of foreignising heavily.

Your discussion of ethnocentric and non-ethnocentric translation in the Ethics part of your paper seems very problematic to me. Perhaps the translator's intention is not ethnocentric, or the critic's reading is not ethnocentric, but, as you say, all these translations are assimilative anyway. Maybe a better word would be ethnocentrifugal which would denote movement or direction, becoming non-ethnocentric. An example which might relate to that would be the reaction of some Mexicans I spoke to about the title of a translated book *Like water for chocolate*. Not only does that not mean anything in English, but it also perpetuates a stereotype, a quaint, picturesque, Hispanic mind or mentality. Take also the translation of a Spanish phrase which is translated literally as 'the world is a handkerchief'. This should be translated as 'it's a small world', but instead this foreignising translation is used to perpetuate condescending, first world stereotypes about a third world culture. So here we have an example of what is intended to be a non-ethnocentric, ethnocentrifugal translation which can be read as being extremely ethnocentric.

Mona Baker (UMIST/University of Middlesex): This is like the phrase 'the mother of all battles' which was used during the Gulf War. This was in fact a literal translation from Arabic which provided a convenient stereotype. So, literalism is not always a good way of being non-ethnocentric.

Lawrence Venuti: An important point here is the context in which any translation strategy is developed. By context I mean at least two things: I mean the context within the text, within the translation and also the context within the target culture. The question of ethnocentricity generally depends on what the current stereotypes are. I'm not suggesting that there's any way out of stereotypes or any way out of representation. Foreignising can only be measured in terms of what previously existed in the culture. So there's a big difference between Yoshimoto and Tom Clancy — we're not getting Japan-bashing from Yoshimoto.

At the same time, I would want to look at what kinds of Japanese terms are left in. If it's a term like 'shogun' or 'karate', we can talk about degrees of familiarisation. One of the things about Yoshimoto is that most of the terms are to do with food and the reader would really have to know Japanese cuisine to understand these terms. So, they have a kind of opacity for Americans who don't frequent Japanese restaurants. That's one way of foreignising.

The context within which the translation works is very important in defining what is foreignising. Of great importance here is the nature of the text and what the translator is doing, for example, what range of translation discourses is employed. Another very important issue here is the idea of culture, the cultural context. As I've already suggested, translations can be mobilised in many different ways and reviewers who are teachers are very important in helping readers respond to texts. Now not every reviewer of the Yoshimoto novel *Kitchen* responded in the way I did, which is to say that readers are bringing assumptions to these texts and often they're not assumptions a translator makes. So what you will find in many cases is readers objecting to the colloquialism in the translation. But I'm suggesting there are other ways to describe this, and this points to the larger problem of the way reviewers treat translations. They tend only to look at stylistic features and they're only interested in one style that needs to be the standard dialect of current English. Anything that deviates from that, generally tends to be classified as a bad translation. Or, put another way, reviewers don't want to be aware of the book as a translation. They prefer the translator to be invisible and anything that makes them aware of the book as a translation tends to be dismissed. Sometimes reviewers don't know what to make of specific formulations they come across. Or the reviewer wants to assimilate the translation to dominant cultural norms or literary style. My main point is that translators need to develop a kind of schizo-ethnicity, that they need to see what's turning them into cultural machines and try to create something that follows deviations. But it's always against what already exists; it's always strategic. I don't want to see the translator as just deciding what is needed in terms of translation discourses, but also which foreign texts should be translated at any one moment. So, there is never a situation where any translation move is going to rectify every omission or exclusion — just the opposite, it's going to create new ones. But, the translator can go off on his tangents and that's the kind of thing that interests me.

Douglas Robinson: What I wanted to point out about your paper was a kind of essentialism. The text has a certain quality — a translation is ethnocentric or it isn't ethnocentric and I'm thinking that, socially speaking, it's a lot more complex than that. We assign certain functional values to texts in different contexts, different eras, different social groups etc.

Lawrence Venuti: But that's my argument. That's the idea of the contingent ethics. It aims to argue against essentialism. The idea of the translator as a strategist is really the way to move against any assumption of essential identity for foreign texts. So that when I say that the translator should develop foreignising strategies, I don't have a particular idea of what's foreign. What is foreign can only be measured against domestic conventions, so it's already a domestication. Translation always introduces a cultural difference. You can't expect a translation to give you the foreign text or to represent in some immediate kind of way an ethnic identity — that's essentialism.

Loredana Polezzi (Warwick University): If you went on with that argument — the essentialist argument — you would end up with a sort of rephrased argument about faithfulness against unfaithfulness, where faithfulness is no longer to the text but to the culture, faithfulness would follow up with stereotypes. But you would end up with that sort of dichotomy again.

Lawrence Venuti: It would push concepts of fidelity to a higher level, so that translators would be interested in what I'm calling a cultural restoration. For example the canon of 20th century Italian Poetry in English does not represent the major lights in Italy; that canon really highlights Eugene Montale. So, all the post-War experimentalist poets, for example Milo De Angelis have all been excluded in English or they've been marginalised because they're only published by small presses.

Loredana Polezzi: Your Yoshimoto example was interesting in that sense, because it is interesting that we should be thinking in terms of traditional canons although she would not fit into these. What was happening in the book was that the two cultures were exchanging things and Yoshimoto is quite explicit and, also, the text they were trying to translate was written by someone between the Japanese and American cultures — so it wants to be translated, but it doesn't want to be translated at the same time. You're saying that every time we translate, we create difference, but at the same time, that difference reflects back. So, it's virtually impossible, I suppose, to distinguish the Mexican image of *Like Water for Chocolate* from the international product that it has become — and to keep them separate. It would seem a terribly difficult thing to do.

Douglas Robinson: But there is no such thing as 'the' Mexican response.

Loredana Polezzi: Exactly. And how do you keep these responses apart and naturally oppose them and say you shouldn't use this one? It seems to be an old argument of fidelity to me.

Lawrence Venuti: Fidelity to the text, or fidelity to the lies?

Loredana Polezzi: Fidelity to something else. As you were saying, pushing it up to some level — fidelity to the text as an artefact and as an expression of a particular identity — so the identity becomes the untouchable, rather than the text. A second level of untouchability.

Douglas Robinson: This rhetoric of fidelity is dealt with in the paper where you say, 'a non-ethnocentric translation project would make available' — not would *construct*, but make available. In other words, something is there and the translator is going to make it available — 'both the exotic and the Americanised' etc.

... 'by restoring those segments', not *some* segments, but *those* segments; not recreating, not construing, but *restoring*. In other words, those things exist, they haven't been made available and the translator is going to come along and take those things and make them available. That's really a rhetoric on fidelity and there's an essentialism there that still hasn't been realised.

Lawrence Venuti: Well, I think something you're assuming then is a kind of ultra-scepticism, that maybe readers shouldn't assume that there is anything out there. But I wouldn't go that far and I would side with Anthony Pym's position that translators are really intercultural subjects because they know things about two cultures. So, I would want to say there are definitely novels in the Japanese tradition — comic novels, or westernised novels — they really exist. It's important for translation to be imagined as a two-step process at least, which is to say the choice of a foreign text is extremely important; the choice of the text is the first ethical move and unfortunately it's not a choice that technical translators can make, ultimately, because they have to decide between eating and translating. In the case of technical translation, this choice has already been made and it's a choice to underwrite economic exchange. But literary translators do have this choice to a certain extent. I think that in the immediate post-War period maybe they didn't have it, that many of the leading translators like Richard Howard, Ralph Mannheim, William Weaver, Helen Lane did not have to propose their projects to publishers. But it seems to me that translators need to think more and more about this choice and you can't think about choice unless you make an estimate of what's out there. Now I'm willing to agree that's an interpretation and if we have an intercultural interpreter — someone who's living in both cultures to a certain extent — that decision is going to be influenced by the two cultures. Again, it would be a strategic move, a contingent move. But I want to say that when I translate, there are these Italian words in the text, what they mean is something that I can recreate in my translation. So, I want to draw the line at a certain point. I'm not interested in free play with the signifier — I wouldn't want to go along with Derrida, but I think partly because I'm interested in politics. If you want to be ultra-sceptical, if you want to release the signifier into freeplay, you can take a stand; to have a political agenda, you must take a stand, you must say something means something.

Foreignising versus Domesticating

Sue Wright (Aston University): You say 'foreignising' and as somebody working outside this area, I'm trying to understand and I don't. Wouldn't it be better to say 'de-foreignising'?

Lawrence Venuti: In what sense?

Sue Wright: You're not making it foreign, you're failing to de-foreignise. To leave the word in the original is surely not to foreignise, it's to fail to de-foreignise.

Lawrence Venuti: Well, no. Foreignising is only something that can be measured in terms of domestic cultural norms.

Sue Wright: In fact when someone says you're foreignising the text, what you're actually failing to do is interpret the text. It's a question of prestige and hierarchy. If you feel that this makes it sound folklorish or stereotyped, than in some way this is not giving it the status it would have in the target language — I don't understand that. It seems to me that there's a prestige, a hierarchy that you're introducing into the debate.

Lawrence Venuti: I'm missing where translation fits into your question.

Sue Wright: You say that the translator is foreignising the text when s/he fails to translate a word into the target language.

Lawrence Venuti: No, that isn't always the case.

Jeremy Maule (Cambridge University): It's not necessarily failing to translate a word, but a deliberate choice, and these are all rather different choices.

Sue Wright: Yes, but my point is still valid. What you're doing is not translating, you're not de-foreignising.

Christina Schäffner (Aston University): That relates to how you define translation and translation strategies. When you differentiate between two main strategies, foreignising and domestication, then making the choice not to come up with an English word is an example of foreignising.

Peter Newmark (University of Surrey): You're introducing the foreign idiolect into the translation. But it's still translation, whether it's syntactical or lexical.

Sue Wright: But if that's seen in any way as stereotyping, then there's a different question. Because then you're introducing the question of hierarchy, of prestige. That to leave it like that is in some way to detract from the text and I find that a very interesting point.

Lawrence Venuti: To detract from which text?

Douglas Robinson: You mean that he's not de-foreignising the source text. Whereas Lawrence was talking about foreignising the target text, foreignising English.

Sue Wright: Yes, I do understand. But I'm pushing this point because I think it is valid. You're talking about foreignising because let's say some of the words in the translated text have remained as they were in the original.

Loredana Polezzi: I think the point about hierarchy and prestige is interesting. Take, for example, the amount of English — idioms or single lexical items — which is left in the translation of a text from English into another language. Or, for that matter, the amount of English in a text which is written in another language. I know one example which is a two part book written by an Italian author as a correspondence from America. The first part is written in the Sixties and hardly any English appears. The second part is written in the 1970s and there is a very large amount of English in the text — that has to do with prestige in my opinion. Call it prestige, hegemony, whatever you want. And it may work the other way around as well. How much Japanese is acceptable in the English text may be a question of the translator's strategic choice or it may be a judgement of the translator as to how much Japanese is acceptable in the 1990s for the American audience.

Terry Hale (University of East Anglia): You said that it was mainly food terms that were left in Japanese in the novel. The problem is that food in Japan is much more than just food. In his book *The Empire of the Senses* Barthes claimed that at the heart of Japan there is an unsignified, an emptiness and meaninglessness which is typified by food. If you think of Anglo-Saxon habits, we cut food and we divide it and we eat it. Whereas there's a more holistic approach to food in Japan and the way they cook and serve it is almost fundamental to the 'Japaneseness' of Japan. And to leave the Japanese food terms untranslated strikes me as a very interesting strategy — it's saying that this is something quintessential about Japan. And, I'd be quite interested to know how these were contextualised — how the scene in a restaurant or at home is described.

Lawrence Venuti: The scenes are at home mostly — there's a lot of take-away! But I should say that not every food term is left in the original language. Food is definitely a metaphor in this book. Food gives comfort and consolation and of course there is the whole idea of comfort food. And it's important for people to be cooking and eating constantly. The thing about leaving in these Japanese terms is that this decision also selects an audience for the novel. I've said this already and it seems important to reiterate the point that not everyone goes to a Japanese restaurant and even people who do go to Japanese restaurants do not know the names of foods, or people may go to Japanese restaurants where everything is translated. So it's selecting a well-educated audience of young people — roughly the same age as the people in the book. The idea that this book is appealing to a certain segment of American culture is important.

Terry Hale: And it's also appealing to a certain lifestyle.

Lawrence Venuti: Yes, that too.

Jean-Pierre Mailhac (University of Salford): Is it really deliberately appealing to a definite culture? What is the alternative? Is the translator going to launch into an explanation of each individual item in every sentence? It's not possible, so the translator doesn't really have a choice.

Lawrence Venuti: But translators do have choices.

Jean-Pierre Mailhac: But you end up with some very strange alternatives. To a certain extent it is not just choice of readership and constituency and so on that results in the translator being forced linguistically to make the whole thing disappear or to stick to the original words.

Lawrence Venuti: Sure, yes, leaving the original words is just more economical, more elegant. But as for the point about translators explaining these terms, well, there have been long traditions of this. So, for example, instead of annotating with a footnote or an endnote that might disrupt the whole reading process, translators have brought the footnote into the text and have omitted the foreign word or put in something that constitutes a definition.

Loredana Polezzi: Or put in a substitution. I can assure you that the muffins in Oscar Wilde's *The Importance of being Earnest* are not muffins in Italian. Instead the term is substituted with what was felt to be the nearest Italian food system equivalent and, of course, in doing this, the translator failed to translate the social class implications. And if you choose to annotate, you are selecting a particular type of reader, so it's again a question of audience.

Douglas Robinson: Yes. Eugene Nida said one should never annotate — he was thinking of a particular type of reader.

Loredana Polezzi: And often these decisions about annotating are editorial decisions with a view to the target audience.

Editorial Limitations

Jeremy Maule (Cambridge University): I'd like to take up this point about editorial intervention. Something I find very interesting in Lawrence's paper — as someone who works mainly with bibliography — is the sort of reception-oriented tone which he's taking. He's directing us to think a lot about reception, publication and copyright and he's taking his research figures from best-seller lists, sales figures, prizes and all the literary systems in which translations move. He asks us to consider the conservative or transgressive effects of translations as depending partly on the strategies of the translator and partly on all these other things which I'll call bibliography. My question then is, given that whole system or market into which you see these texts moving, how contingent are the contingent ethics of the translator? You seem to see literary translators as free authorial spirits and yet at the same time your paper is appropriately worrying about the sociology of reception.

Lawrence Venuti: First of all, the idea of looking at publishing history and at reception is very important to me. This was one of the anti-essentialist moves. I am not assuming that these foreign texts, whether in the foreign language or in translation, have some inherent meaning. What I'm really interested in is seeing how translation effects register with editors and reviewers. This is important when deciding whether the strategy employed by the translator is domesticating or foreignising. Often when the translator is not mentioned at all you can be sure there's been a thorough domestication — maybe I shouldn't say 'sure', but there's a strong likelihood. Most reviewers, as I've mentioned, prefer translators to be invisible.

As for your second point about what happens to the translator as strategist, one of the consequences of looking at translation as a different kind of authorship is that it causes you to think differently about authorship. For decades now we've been under a kind of Romantic conception of authorship, where the text is a form of self-expression and the materials in the text are self-originating, and the whole act of composition is self-determining in a basic way. I look at the translator as dealing with materials that pre-exist the act of translation in his/her own culture. For the foreignising translator this is very important because you have these two sets of determinants. You have a cultural matrix out there — a tendency on the part of reviewers to respond in a certain way towards translations or on the part of publishers or editors to commission or edit translations in a certain way. But you also have the entire tradition of the English language. The translator cannot be said to have determined any of these things, but these are the determinants that shape the translator's work. The translator needs to get a sense of where translation is at any one moment — this is what I mean by the translator as strategist — and then decide, on the basis of this assessment, what foreign text should be translated. Also, what range of English language discourses should be selected. So, I'm looking at the translator as a particular kind of author who does not so much originate a text but produces a text by selecting materials from a certain tradition and arranges them in a certain order of priority and elaborates them in the translation. So that's the idea of avoiding the romantic concept of authorship.

Jeremy Maule: If you put this order of priority across a spectrum, then I guess that at one end of the spectrum would be a move that doesn't just translate but gives you the entire foreign language text and the translation in every point. Is this as far as you would go?

Lawrence Venuti: Well, it was Ezra Pound who claimed that there were two types of translation. The translation he called a new work of art and which he published as his texts — *The Seafarer* for example — without calling them translations. Then there was another kind of translation that he called interpretative translation or translation of accompaniment. And for me what he did in his translations could be a kind of foreignising strategy. He insisted that these would have a bilingual publication and what he described as the atrocities of mistranslation would drive the reader across the page to the foreign language text. So, the reader was facing the foreign language text and the translation. The translation had priorities that were foreignising in two senses, namely in that they disturbed English language cultural norms and simultaneously forced the reader to confront the foreign language. For example, he would use archaic registers and these are what he called his atrocities. So, bilingual publication is a possibility, but the nature of foreign language study today means that the translation replaces the foreign language text completely. And there is a real problem because we cannot do bilingual publications in an English language culture right now, especially not in the USA, where foreign language study is still very marginal. For example, it's very difficult for foreign language Ph.D.s to find jobs, many universities have abandoned foreign language departments, plus there's a low translation rate. So, translation in this kind of situation becomes one point of intervention, one place where the concept of cultural difference can be circulated. But it's a difficult problem.

Peter Bush (University of Middlesex): What strikes me is that you're excessively rationalistic when you talk about choices translators can and can't make. I don't think that when you translate you make choices in the rationalistic way you describe. I also think that your opposition between domestic and foreign is too absolute. If you start from the position that the translator has got a material consciousness which is multicultural or bicultural, you have to realise that even the monocultural is quite heterogeneous. If you look at what's being written in Anglo-Saxon cultures at present, a lot of it contains non-English words and concepts, for example, Salman Rushdie in the British context and, Laura Esquivel in the United States, whose work is full of Spanish references which the standard American reader might not understand, but her work sells.

Lawrence Venuti: On your first point about how rationalistic this method is: for me, translating is very much a process of discovery. I've translated books that I didn't read completely before beginning to translate them, and I prefer that, actually, over knowing what's in store. Not knowing this, forces the development of a translation strategy to be an on-going process, worked out in the translating, and so there's a serendipity involved. Of course translators usually come to projects with a more developed sense of possible strategies; I'm just saying that with any project, a more rigorously considered approach, based on an awareness of which texts in a foreign literature have already been translated and what kind of strategies have been used to translate them — this sort of thinking needn't eliminate discovery or invention, that I believe occurs in any writing, including translation. And it can take different forms. My recent projects have focused on a 19th century writer of Gothic tales, Tarchetti, whose work immediately suggested the use of archaism. Making this decision, however, didn't determine every move I would make as a translator. I still had to decide what archaisms to use and where. While translating I read a Gothic classic, Bram Stoker's *Dracula*, and drew up lists of words and phrases, many of which I later incorporated into the project. My Tarchetti translations really weren't finished when the proofs were sent to the printer.

On the second point: How absolute is the distinction between domestic and foreign? I want to make it clear that translation is fundamentally domestication. It's one culture appropriating texts from another culture — there's also an element of dehistoricisation there. Translation is part of an imperialist move and the question is: How can we compensate for it?, that is, compensate for readers who do not know the foreign language.

Translation Strategies

Said Faiq (University of Salford): You said that you would like to give the translator the role of a type of author and you talked a lot about translation strategies and translation discourses. But I wanted to know what you meant by strategies. If these strategies remain individualistic, differing between one person and another, then translation studies will never become an independent, respected academic discipline. The thinking will still be that if you know two languages you can translate. A lot of the study of discourse has been concerned with studying writing, that is text production in the first place, and again the problem is: How original is the original? I think that the reception phase for the translator is the same as for any other reader. But for the general reader, the actual activity stops there — s/he can interpret the text in his/her own way. But the translator at the end of the receiving phase assumes the role of re-drafter of that source text into the target text, the target culture, target semiotics. I think translation has to be seen as a semiotic activity — not in terms of a narrow definition of signifier and signified prevalent within literary criticism. If we see translation as a semiotic activity, we could develop strategies for doing translation and then at least the translator could defend him/herself and a review could then be backed up by a theoretical framework rather than just being based on personal opinion.

Lawrence Venuti: Firstly, how individualistic would these strategies be — these foreignising strategies? I think it's important to recognise that translation is a form of writing, and in the same way that the most interesting writing is not machine-produced or uniform, I don't think we should expect the translator to develop some uniform approach to every text. I would insist again on the strategic nature of developing translation discourses. Often what is happening is that the translator is developing a concept of equivalence during the process. Now the concept of equivalence is generally an interpretation. We're not talking about a one-to-one correspondence — there'll always be a disjunction, but we're talking about a translation, a replacement of the text. But the translator is not developing the discourse out of some sort of vacuum. It's not individualistic in that sense, it's possessive individualism, it's really a matter of being aware of what materials are available to you as a writer in the English language and I think these materials have a wide historical range. So it's not individualistic in any philosophical sense, but there will definitely be peculiarities. Translators, given specific projects, may develop specific strategies, but I don't see why we have to systematise them at the level you're suggesting, since then we'd be requiring translators to adopt the same moves in each case.

The second point: Is this too much literary criticism? Well, it's definitely influenced by literary cultural theory, but it's also discourse analysis. I guess if discourse analysts want to look at translation, they should develop their own theories. This is a theory of culture that can be useful to translators and also to students of translation. I guess it's also a question of picking your theory, and the methodological framework I'm coming from is the post-structuralist framework with a very heavy dose of the Marxist tradition of the Frankfurt School. I'm very interested in cultural theory, as opposed to a scientific analysis. The latter can be dangerous in many of these cases because I think it's likely to develop universal laws, and what is a general theory will be applied across the board. So, I'm interested in a general theory, but one that allows for enough flexibility so that different translators working in different languages can develop different translation strategies depending on the moment they're working in.

Mona Baker: Most people think of translation strategies in terms of a pedagogical tool, turning translators into machines. But you must first learn how to use a language so that you can manipulate it and really do exciting translations.

Said Faiq: By strategies, I mean that you can train people to become better text handlers. Because if they are better text handlers at the receiving end, then at least their interpretations of that text would be 90% reliable.

Mona Baker: There's no such thing as a reliable interpretation, surely.

Said Faiq: There can be, within an overall discourse theory.

Lawrence Venuti: This is the problem. Canons of accuracy in translation are historically determined — that's a basic assumption of mine. Which is to say that what was 'accurate' for translations from Latin in the 18th century may not be accurate for translation today. And, at the same time, publishers are holding translators to a great degree of accuracy today. Most translator's contracts — at least in the United States — will have a special clause which guarantees that this is original work, that nothing has been omitted and that it's accurate. But the concept of accuracy — what I'm calling the canon of accuracy, the standard by which it is judged — is unspecified, and for many translators this is a trap, since it invites the publisher to say that it is inaccurate, and the publisher then may decide to have it rewritten. But I think there are scholarly canons of accuracy, there are book market canons of accuracy and they vary widely, even in one moment. So, I'm reluctant to pursue this argument because of where it would go in the end, which is towards a more scientific theory and into philosophical semantics. That could produce very interesting work on translation — I don't want to suggest that it wouldn't, but, for me, we're moving further and further away from translators who will not have the expertise to dip into philosophical semantics — not in 1995 — and also we're getting further away from readers, who are not going to apply standards of accuracy and publishers who are not going to be interested in philosophical semantics. So I think, yes, there is a place for a more scientific, systematic study of translation, but how this would actually fit into a translation studies curriculum or a translation training programme or the publishing industry generally — these are questions which need to be answered.

Christina Schäffner: But we can make a difference between literary and non-literary texts. Quite a lot of research has been done in the field of non-literary texts to find out text-typological conventions. And in the case of highly conventionalised texts, one could actually develop a kind of strategic advice for the translator.

Said Faiq: What I meant was a kind of general overall framework for translation practice, starting with establishing appropriate and efficient strategies for text reception and for taking the text into the target language. I mean overall strategies, not actual choices at the level of words, phrases, structures. After all, language doesn't make sense, we make sense of language, and the choices and systems are there for everyone to choose from.

The Validity of the Narcissistic Concept

Peter Newmark: I'd like to introduce a new subject which worries me and which you mentioned in your paper. You say 'Translation forms domestic subjects by enabling a process of mirroring or self-recognition'. This seems to me a terribly dogmatic statement. There is of course some mirroring, but the way you put it, it's as if this is all translators do and that the process of translation is basically narcissistic. I think that's untrue. It suggests that in reading you are admiring yourself in Shylock, Othello or whoever. There may be some truth in this, but there's no qualification at all in your statement: 'The reader identifies with an ideal projected by the translation, usually values that have achieved authority'. But often it's just the opposite — they haven't. Are you talking about moral authority or power authority or what in the domestic culture? It's an over-simplification and it's dangerous. And there are no absolutes in translation, let alone in commentaries on translation. I think you should be more cautious.

Lawrence Venuti: This is an important issue. The theoretical assumptions with regard to subject formation are partly psychoanalytic.

Peter Newmark: But that's deplorable!

Lawrence Venuti: The consequences of psychoanalysis were partly concepts of ideology, I'm thinking of the kinds of synthesis in psychoanalysis in the Marxist tradition of Louis Althusser who sees the subject as recognising him/herself in a role created by an institution — the Church, the State or the School. I think that in most translations something similar happens in the sense that in order for the translation to be intelligible and to make sense to the reader, the translation needs to seem familiar to a certain extent.

Peter Newmark: That's a truism.

Lawrence Venuti: Okay. Now this familiarity can only be built on the basis of target culture allusions, which is to say allusions to the reader's own culture — here's the element of narcissism. The basis of intelligibility for the reader is really a kind of sampling of domestic cultural values. Yet, there's obviously more going on and any translation of a foreign text *is* still a foreign text. Then there's the whole thematic level and so forth. But I think that there is this process of self-recognition — that's how people understand one another, there is a kind of basic familiarity.

Peter Newmark: But why do you call it narcissism, which means admiring oneself?

Lawrence Venuti: I think that's a kind of narrow Freudian definition, that the subject identifies with a kind of ego-ideal.

Douglas Robinson: It's not about admiration. It's about constructing the self through identification with another. So, it's not *liking* the other thing but *recognising* it as familiar, as something that is outside yourself, but also already inside yourself as well.

Peter Newmark: But can't you get away from the word narcissism?

Douglas Robinson: It's not like Narcissus in the Greek myth, it's not so much about admiration as about unstable ego-structure because it's based on identification with someone outside the self.

Peter Newmark: I know that.

Douglas Robinson: So we're not talking about self-love.

Peter Newmark: But I'm talking about the reader of a translation.

Douglas Robinson: Lawrence is trying to create a social-psychological model of the process of how familiar-sounding translations are created and I think that narcissism is an excellent model or metaphor for this, although it may not represent exactly what happens.

Lawrence Venuti: The question of identifying with an ideal in the culture is very important. This case-study of the Japanese fiction really bears that out — the fact that very prestigious publishers were repeatedly publishing the same authors meant that this then became for the readers the standard by which all Japanese literature was judged. This meant that readers were reading these novels and essentially identifying with a dominant cultural value that had motivated the translation of these Japanese texts in the first place. It happened for 40 years, from the 1950s until the translation of texts by Yoshimoto. So what we had then were these two generations of readers and often the same translators were creating these two generations with a very defined taste for Japanese fiction. This involved, I think, a process of recognising the familiar, recognising the next Japanese writer who came along because s/he was recognisable in terms of the writers who had already been translated. I'm really interested in the way translation can shape consciousness, the way culture forms consciousness, admitting of course that the process is not complete. I'm not a functionalist, although texts can create positions for readers to occupy. If you understand a text, there's got to be some point in that text from which intelligibility comes. As soon as you get to that point, you've occupied a position, not only a position of intelligibility, but also a position in a particular set of values, a hierarchy of values. It's a position of ideology in fact.

Douglas Robinson: You're a functionalist, but you're a static functionalist. You're not interested in systematising or fixing the function in some kind of perfect, systematic way.

Lawrence Venuti: The thing about this functionalism is that it doesn't always lead to social reproductions, that is to a process of repetition and difference. Continual translation, continual reading will create new meanings and I think that's how change is possible.

Peter Newmark: I accept all this. You're going against the whole Skopos School?

Lawrence Venuti: I think so. I'd like to qualify some of the functionalism of the whole Skopos theory, by taking into consideration the fact that texts can be used for multiple functions. Or, the motive depends on what a reader brings to a text. A reader may resist the position of intelligibility or identification created for him or her — readers do it all the time, when they don't like translations. It's not like the reader is sutured in a position, although this term, 'sutured', has been used to describe this. I think it's a process where stitches are missed.

Translation and the Market

Terry Hale: I like very much this idea of mirroring or self-recognition and its importance in translation. If I were asked when the lowest ebb of translation in this country was, I would say in the 1930s, 1940s and 1950s, and it strikes me that this was the time when we were actually developing, very actively, a consciousness of English literature as a tradition which had its own rules, which wasn't influenced by the continent or anybody else and there was an absolute denial of seeing ourselves in other cultures and this was the moment when translation worked the least well. And it basically came down to Leavis in this country — he didn't like Joyce, because he thought Joyce was a ruthless avant-garde. He didn't like texts which dealt with changes in sexual identity because he had very traditional values in this area. And so there was a wholesale rejection of what was happening in contemporary European culture and, essentially, we didn't participate in this country. The United States also seemed to have a low ebb about the same time. Was there some kind of nationalistic force which worked against translation at the same period?

Lawrence Venuti: This is an interesting point. I think translation in the United States has, for centuries, been a cultural practice which has enacted the colonisation, the dispossession and assimilation of people whose native languages were not English. And I think that during the great wave of immigration, say from 1870 to 1920, there was great pressure put on immigrants to assimilate. For example, on Ellis Island, interpreters had about six languages and there was also a system of language schools developed for immigrants. In other words, there was a repression of cultural difference. I don't have the translation statistics for those years, I don't know if they even exist. But I know that probably the heyday for translation in the United States was the early 1960s. I think the 1930s were more varied at different levels, there was much more attention given to European cultural developments. But I think there was great pressure put on the great waves of industrial workers from Europe to assimilate, to give up their language and, ultimately, what that meant was giving up translations. Now today, according to the latest census of the United States, 39 million out of about 250 million inhabitants speak a language other than English at home. So there is tremendous diversity in American culture still, also at the level of language. Now the automatic tellers in banks run in English, Spanish, Greek, Chinese and Korean. At the same time, I think today there is this wave of xenophobia and one form it's taking is an effort to stamp out bilingual education.

Said Faiq: Taking up again the point about function. After all, texts do emerge within particular societies or cultures, and these cultures and societies are typically dominated by relations of power, conflicts and cohesion. I personally would like to see the text as having a, let's say, macro-function which is then served by some micro-functions within it, because if it is multifunctional, we lose the text. Normally, the reviewer of a translation will say this book is about, for example, love and power in 20th century Japan or whatever and that's it. That is the macro-function and then it is served by other sub-texts within the text.

Lawrence Venuti: Translation is generally a problem of decontextualisation. You take a text from a foreign culture and you translate it. If other texts from that culture haven't been translated then it's a drop in the ocean. You can't expect your reader to have the cultural resources to make sense of the text. In the end, readers will do what they want and you can't do anything to stop the various uses to which translations will be put. The idea of the translator intervening in a recognisable way in order to shape the response to the text — well that's problematic too. You need educated readers, readers who are willing to say 'this is a translation and I can see it in the text'. But I think the most you can do is try to be aware of what literatures are underrepresented or misrepresented or whether there is an unequal representation of certain writers from certain foreign cultures. It depends on translators who are not just sitting back and waiting for commissions, but who are willing to be aggressive and to be truly intercultural in their approach to publishers.

Problems of Dichotomies

Jean Pierre Mailhac: Could I come back to the concept of ethnocentricity, which is obviously quite central to your argument. I thoroughly enjoyed reading your paper and found it very interesting. But looking at your definition of ethnocentricity, where you come up with examples, I seem to feel there's a sort of mismatch. You say that ethnocentric translation, generally under the guise of transmissibility, carries out a systematic negation of the strangeness of the foreign word. Then you give us the Japanese translation as an example. Yet it seems to me that what happened with that Japanese text is the exact opposite. You criticised the fact that the translator over-emphasised the Japanese cultural emblem and ignored the Western part. So it's not a systematic negation of the Japanese cultural identity, but it's over-emphasising something which is more essentially Japanese and less Western. It seems to me that there is a certain tension between your definition and this example. Also, the non-ethnocentric project is supposed to be an opening, a dialogue of cross-breeding and decentering and it seems to me that these people were trying to re-establish the dialogue with the Japanese culture which had broken down. Similarly, the example of the Greek text. You say it's non-ethnocentric, because it's not based on an Anglo-American canon of romantic Greece, so in that sense it's non-ethnocentric. But then you also say it was based on Nietzsche, on Heidegger, on existentialism. These are not Greek cultural heirlooms, so it still seems to be ethnocentric, it's just that a third party has got involved and this happens to be kinder to the original culture and to introduce fewer distortions. So although the original culture has come through better, it's still not the source culture, it's not the target culture, it's a third one. In that sense it's not really non-ethnocentric.

Lawrence Venuti: No, and that's a very important point. The thing is that ethnocentrism, like domestication in this paper, is gauged against the domestic culture. Or, even more specifically, a non-ethnocentric approach to translation depends on finding values that are not currently dominant in the domestic culture. So the assumption is, there's a hierarchy of values in the domestic culture, some are dominant, some are marginal etc. And, since all translation is fundamentally domestication and is really initiated in the domestic culture, there is, therefore, a fundamental ethnocentric impulse in all translation. The question then becomes: How do you measure your project against the reigning stereotype? With the Japanese example, I think there are two issues involved here. These Japanese writers were chosen because they reflected what American readers were interested in reading about Japan — not the militaristic Japan, but a previous Japan. So, here is the first ethnocentric move. Here is a post-War culture, that enabled the dissemination of Japanese fiction in the United States, but what happened is that it hardened into a stereotype. The second move is that subsequent translations were assimilated to what I'm calling this canon, this hardened stereotype. A process of familiarisation took place and this was maintained consistently. So, there are two kinds of ethnocentrism here. One is that foreign texts are always put to domestic uses — even if only to learn more about the foreign culture. There are economic interests at work here too and the interests served by translations are, at a crucial stage, domestic and it's hard to get rid of that — that's the basic ethnocentric move. However, once you admit that, how can you then open up a space for something that's less ethnocentric and that would be an attempt to revise dominant cultural values — what we currently think of as Japanese fiction, or what we currently think of as Greek tragedy. And it's that change that I'm getting at when I'm talking about foreignising. Now, often what happens is that this change in the representation of a foreign culture is precipitated by things that happen at home. That is something which seems to me happened with John Jones and Aristotle's *Poetics*. Here was a British classicist who came up with a very different approach to Greek tragedy, an approach that deviated from the tradition of the very individualistic in England. He did it because there were other foreign cultural forms being imported — for example, existentialism. These were foreign, but they weren't Greek. So, it was an influx of other foreign cultures that enabled Jones to refocus on Greek texts. That strikes me as a very interesting example, because it shows the complexity of the processes.

Jean-Pierre Mailhac: But what you're calling ethnocentric is the act of wanting to read something about Japan. That could equally be called non-ethnocentric. So there's a contradiction here and I think the problem may be that your definition is not the same as Douglas'. Because it's not a systematic negation.

Lawrence Venuti: You're right. And as my paper goes on, those initial points about basic domestication or ethnocentrism in translation get minimalised and I set up the dichotomy between domestication and foreignising but it doesn't always admit the extent to which foreignising also has this domesticating impulse in it.

Douglas Robinson: Ethnocentricity and non-ethnocentricity and domestication and foreignisation assume different functions at different stages in a historical process. In your paper you talked about translation being a process of decontextualisation and that translation always dehistoricises a text, which bothers me because it seems that contextuality and historicity are essential qualities in the foreign text which are then lost. I prefer *re*historicisation, *re*contextualisation which suggest an ongoing process and a move away from a myth of a loss of historicity or contextuality, a move to that semiotic process which I think is directed in different ways by different social processes. What we're talking about here is not dehistoricity but being caught up in the flow of historicity and deciding which way you're going.

Lawrence Venuti: The thing about decontextualisation and dehistoricisation is that these are terms which try to admit that essentially we have two historical rhythms here — the foreign culture and the domestic culture and that these are not simultaneous. And the assumption is that when you translate a text, a lot depends for the reception of that text on what access to knowledge about the foreign culture is available in the domestic culture. And, with many literary translations, depending on what literature it is, there's often very little. Now, with scholarly translations I think it's a different case — there is a context there, but it's not the same context as the foreign culture. So, I'm using the de- instead of re- to emphasise the disjunction.

Peter Newmark: I hope you won't let go of your reference to dehistoricisation, because it's very valuable. A sudden exposure of a text to a foreign language and a foreign culture is often like a breath of cold air. You see it, not in the light of this culture or that culture but in terms of common sense — the universal that you probably don't recognise, but I do. Dehistoricisation is exactly what happens and what Douglas said about rehistoricisation is also true, but that comes later.

Peter Bush: Your definition of the domestic and the foreign is too much posited on nationalism. For example, in Germany, you've got a new literary culture developing in the form of literature written by Turkish immigrants, but publishers aren't interested in translating these books into English, because the conservative British establishment that Terry was talking about says no. I consider myself to be a subversive, aggressive translator, but I find that my main battle is with the literary establishment. It's so soaked in Leavisite Englishness.

Peter Newmark: Could you explain that remark?

Peter Bush: Well, the particular tradition of seeing English literature as the centre of moral values and literary worth.

Peter Newmark: That's not Leavisite Englishness. I'm speaking as a student of Leavis and I feel it's my duty to defend him.

Peter Bush: I was educated by Leavisites through Grammar School and University and I've had to fight against this in order to develop a voice as a translator. I tried to get these translations of Turkish-German literature published, and they would get to a certain level before the publishers would say they didn't like them. And why not? Because they like a kind of dirty realism, short sentences and that comes back, to a certain extent, to this whole idea of readability, which I think is linked up with Englishness and nationalism.

Terry Hale: But there is obviously a problem, because less than 3% of titles are translated in this country and the United States. Now is this because English is a dominant language or is it because there are some cultural forces at work? Lawrence, I think you're saying that cultural forces are at work to exclude translation.

Lawrence Venuti: Yes, and it's also economic. I think there's a trade imbalance when it comes to publishing translations. Many American and British publishers will go to the big international book markets and fairs and what they will do is sell the rights to translate English language books, but they won't buy the rights to translate foreign language books. So, there is ultimately this imbalance and I don't think imperialism is too strong a word for this. It has kept translation rates in English language countries very low since the 1950s, but it ensures that the American and British global best-sellers are out there, that American or English language values have been sold worldwide and they've created a world market. But they've neglected a market in the United States and Britain and they've created a readership that is aggressively monolingual, that's unreceptive to the foreign unless it's recognisably American or British or unless it can be assimilated to the kinds of national stereotypes that Peter was talking about. It's very hard for foreignising translations to erode that because of publishers and I've had a lot of problems with this. There are two issues here, there's the English language writing that's already there and there are these stereotypes of foreign literature and the attitude is, if it's not Italo Calvino, we're not going to translate it. That's a real problem.

This idea of multi-ethnic literature, for example the Turkish-German situation, is very important. It's hard to get these books translated because of these factors. But, also I think these texts are probably very difficult to translate.

Peter Bush: But, isn't it also true that the generations of students we're teaching at our universities are students that come with that multilingual consciousness? So, when you talk about domestic versus foreign, you're not really representing their experiences. If you present them with this kind of absolute of domestic versus foreign you're not really helping them to grapple with what is their experience and what they want to do.

Lawrence Venuti: Not unless you look at these concepts in terms of dominant cultural values that have excluded them in the first place. And that would be the idea. In order to foreignise translations we need to introduce other kinds of cultural discourses including the ones from their own cultures.

Peter Bush: But I find your statement that all translation is domestication a very negative statement and I have to react against it instinctively. It's like saying you have to be faithful.

Translation and Social Change

Jeremy Maule: This leads me to another point: To what extent can translation cause social change? You talk about translation selecting its audience and being acceptable to that audience, so it seems to me that you're preaching to the converted. To what extent can you have faith that translation can change social norms and values? Or is it just part of the general social process?

Lawrence Venuti: I think a translation of a religious text or of texts that are housed in major social institutions can definitely precipitate social change in a dramatic way. Scholarly translations can precipitate change in terms of a complete restructuring of a discipline and the formation of a new consciousness in the students of that discipline. Something that we haven't mentioned so far is that the readership for literature is relatively small. There is a larger audience for film and television than there is for literature, and the kinds of changes that literary translation can bring about are definitely going to be within a minority of the culture. But then there are these larger social institutions, like the church, and my point about Jerome's Bible translation I had discussed in the paper was to show that translations can cause potentially wide-ranging social changes. Today, we need to think of translation more in terms of electronic media and the relations between dubbing and sub-titling and so on. If we're entirely pessimistic, literature is a dying cultural form, whereas hypertext, interactive videos etc. are on the increase.

Jeremy Maule: You must have a very strong belief in the free word, if you believe that this can come about, just as Stanley Fish has a very deterministic belief, although he has the concept of change built in as well.

Lawrence Venuti: Yes, I think he's very interested in institutions. But I think I have a much more flexible concept of what an institution is. For example, a few years ago, I heard Stanley Fish give a talk entitled 'Interdisciplinarity is so very hard to do'. And his idea was that interdisciplinarity is impossible. That as soon as you import the discourses from another discipline, you're doing another discipline and he raises basic questions about communication. But I happen to think that social relations, social practices are much more heterogeneous — that's how change happens. There's a sense today in which things are highly interdisciplinary, that literary study, for example, has changed dramatically since the 1950s. And things have changed because discourses from other disciplines have been imported into literary criticism. So now there's something interdisciplinary called cultural studies. I guess, coming out of the Marxist tradition, I'm looking for social contradictions everywhere and I'm finding them!

Said Faiq: So, can translation be used intentionally to precipitate social change?

Lawrence Venuti: Well, that's my idea, but I guess I'm a bit too utopian — my pessimism has this utopian set of assumptions!

Julian Edge: Translation in terms of how it's being discussed here is not what I do. But I hear so many resonances in terms of what you're talking about and in terms of what I do, that I'd like to check out a couple of perceptions with you and see how translators respond to those. I'm involved in foreign language teacher education and more specifically education of teachers of English in other parts of the world. What interests me in what you have been talking about is this idea of the intercultural actor, which, I think, is one perfectly authentic image of what these teachers are. The transfer of pedagogic know-how around the world has been carried out, first of all according to a classic Western science theory-application, and secondly, that in itself fuels and is fuelled by a classic centre-periphery model. So the theory is to be learned in the centre and then you take your theories and you go off and apply them — which has proved to be pretty dysfunctional. In a project which seeks to encourage knowledge production and know-how production in places where experience is being had, where the English language is being taught, it seems to me that a properly educational and sociologically developed concept of translation is what is required — in terms of the transfer of pedagogical know-how around the world from these centres, where these different manifestations of this knowledge are taking place. And I'd like to know if that concept resonates at all with anybody whose business is the translation of texts and, if it does, I'd like to push it one step further. It seems to me that a properly developed idea of ethical translation — as in this paper — is also potentially at the heart of a response from the human sciences, from new paradigm sciences to the challenges from the classical Western scientistic approach, in terms of concepts like objectivity, validity, reliability. In the human sciences, these are not to be dealt with in the way that a scientistic approach asks us to. And, in a properly developed concept of translation, how can this meaning find some kind of authentication somewhere else among other people? These are ideas of translation that are important to me in those two ways.

Douglas Robinson: Authentication or recreation?

Julian Edge: I'd step back from recreation because of the retrospective resonance of that particular 're'. I think it will always be a creation anew. The scientistic paradigm always asks us to question, Is this true? Whereas a human science paradigm encourages us to ask the question: What can I learn from this? To me, the concept of translation is resonant with this idea of how this particular form of reality, truth, human experience can be translated so that these people can authentically ask the questions: How can I relate to this? What can I learn from this? It moves away from this misleading question: Is this true?

Jeremy Maule: At the level of the metaphor, it's clear that translation is closer to the human science paradigm, I agree with that.

Douglas Robinson: What you're talking about is the translation for the 'savage'. Like, for example, what happened with the native Americans — this notion of turning people into something. Teaching English as a Foreign Language turns people into intercultural actors.

Mona Baker: In answer to Julian's question about translation as transfer of know-how from one culture to another, Anthony Pym has got a very good book called *Translation and Text Transfer* and he has also written articles about the movement and transfer of know-how through texts. He's also got his own version of the ethics of translation based on the situation that as a translator you are ethically bound to make decisions on behalf of the client — including the decision not to translate but to recommend language learning instead, as a strategy in cases where translation would not be economic and efficient, for example, for a long-term project involving a lot of people. So, he's got his own version of the ethics of translation which he sees as the transfer of texts and know-how across cultures, which seems to tie in with your point.

Practical Options for Implementing these Concepts

Agnes Kukulska-Hulme (Aston University): I wanted to come back to the question of the choice of text to be translated and the idea that the translator should put forward suggestions to publishers. I just wondered if you had any suggestions about the mechanisms of persuasion which translators could use, from your own experience of persuading publishers to take on different projects and texts.

Lawrence Venuti: Dinner helps sometimes! But the point is that publishers look at translation as an inevitable loss in economic terms. So, if you can get a foreign cultural institution involved with a publishing subsidy, the publisher will think twice about a translation. That's a very important step, but it's not always possible. Often I encourage publishers by approaching them with a detailed proposal, a quote and a sample translation. A combination of this, with a very close scrutiny of a publisher's list to see what books the publisher has translated including from the language your book is in. It's a waste of time to try and get a publisher interested in a book or kind of book in which they've shown no interest in the past. Also, you need an opinion-maker who's willing to write reports supporting your proposal — a writer, a translator or someone who has some cultural authority. What generally happens in New York is that 99.5% of publishers know no foreign language — that's another reason why so few translations are published. What they do then is rely on specialist readers who are often translators. However, some publishers are very hesitant to have translators write reader's reports because there is some self-interest involved. It would be better for a foreign language specialist or a foreign writer who has English to write a report. I guess what I'm recommending is very makeshift, but that's the way the situation is.

Loredana Polezzi: But you said earlier that you are in a privileged position in that you can be disruptive. If you are fighting against a canon or an acquired sense of what English texts should look like and so on, it's not so easy. It sounds utopian, I hope it's optimistic.

Lawrence Venuti: True. As a translator I feel very lucky because most of my translations have not come from commissions and I've done crazy things like translating entire books before looking for publishers. With the 19th century writer, Tarchetti, I translated the book on my own and then shopped around and nobody would buy it — not even university presses. It was completely unknown in English, nothing I could do would make it interesting. It was Gothic and I thought I was tapping into a popular interest in Gothic and introducing a new angle, because this was Italian, and there were very interesting things about this writer's career and so on — but nobody was interested. Finally what happened was that an editor who knew my work and who had what he called a neglected classics series published it — so in a way it was an accident.

Peter Newmark: Could you simply explain this sentence from your paper: 'Perhaps the domestic identities formed by translation can avoid the dislocations of the foreign only when institutions regulate translation practices so restrictively [Are you a friend of the French Government?!] as to efface and hence defuse the linguistic and cultural differences of foreign texts'. What are you recommending here and what do you mean?

Lawrence Venuti: Any translation, in so far as it's dealing with foreign culture, is potentially dislocating to the domestic culture. But since translation is often housed in institutions that have some control over the texts that circulate within them, they can regulate the translation process to such an extent that any dislocation produced by foreign cultural terms is minimised.

Peter Newmark: I presume you're against this?

Lawrence Venuti: No, not really. This is in a context here of discussing bible translations. I'm looking at it from the point of view of the church as an institution. But it's clear that some institutions are more conservative than others.

Myriam Carr (University of Salford): I wanted to come back to the selection of texts. I wonder to what extent this criterion or constraint is underestimated in translation discourse and where the history of translation comes in as well. It seems to me that selection is rarely innocent or random — there is always a reason for translating. Two examples would be translations from Greek into Syrian and Arabic in the 9th century where Greek philosophy was translated but not Greek literature because it did not fulfil a need in the target culture. In the same way, when Arabic translations of Greek science and philosophy were further translated into Latin and Spanish, there was some radical selection and whatever was seen as not relevant to the target culture in terms of historical or geographical references was just not translated.

Lawrence Venuti: Well, I think it's exactly as you say — it's always a question of relevance. Except that what constitutes relevance changes historically. Today, to begin at the bottom line, publishers tend to look for translations that could be best-sellers in English. For example, the phenomenon of the tie-in. When Andrew Lloyd-Webber's *Phantom of the Opera* was a success in London and it was planned to bring the show to Broadway, American publishers scrambled to bring out translations of the French novel in English and by the time it opened there were four paperback translations available. So I think the concept of relevance is the key idea — that's a clear-cut example because the relevance is commercial. But I think if you look back over history, cultural needs were definitely served by translation — domestic cultural needs that is. So, ultimately, I think this goes back to the idea of domestication and ethnocentrism; that if we look at translation as a good thing, then we also have to admit that it's a good thing for the domestic culture. And there is, fundamentally, the question of whose interests are being served.

In the long run, I guess the hope is that the more that gets translated, the better — the whole point about the low rates of translation in English rests on this assumption — because you have a more heterogeneous culture that's open to cultural difference. That's the benefit in terms of the domestic culture. In the long term, it may improve geo-political relations or there may be some sort of pay-off for the foreign cultures in that way. But with translation you're taking a chance.

Loredana Polezzi: Do you think the same comments you're making apply if you are not talking from an American point of view? Can you still talk about values in the same way as positive or negative without risking something essentialist or something else?

Lawrence Venuti: No. I think that's an important point. For example some Italian publishers have lists, 90% of which are translations — many of them from English. So what's happening is that you could say these Italian publishers are essentially in collusion with American publishers because they're making an awful lot of money disseminating American culture in Italy. But the reverse is not happening. So are these Italian publishers really serving Italian culture? Are they diversifying it? Well, I think you'd say they're Americanising it.

Douglas Robinson: In Finland, fewer and fewer Finnish books are published every year. Instead the publishers go to the Frankfurt Book Fair and see what sells well in English and translate that into Finnish. So publishers are less and less willing to take a risk on Finnish books and translation is big business at the moment in Finland. But, looked at the other way around: who's going to translate a Finnish novel for an American audience? I could understand these problems with the Finnish language, but it is very interesting to hear that there is the same problem with Italian books.

Terry Hale: I'm not sure that it matters that so much American literature is being translated into Finnish, because there is obviously a group within Finnish society which finds this very fulfilling and interesting. So I think you have to be quite careful here with popular culture, because popular culture has been translated a lot. In the 19th century a vast amount of popular culture was translated into English — something nobody ever talks about and something which would force us to re-evaluate everything that has been said about 19th century literature. There seems to be an assumption that the same piece of popular culture is read in the same way by everyone around the world which is obviously not the case.

Lawrence Venuti: And this is clearly something which translators have to bear in mind.

TRANSLATION AND ADVERTISING: GOING GLOBAL

Candace Séguinot

School of Translation, Glendon College, York University, 2275 Bayview Avenue, Toronto, Ontario, Canada M4N 3M6

Abstract The identity-forming power of translation is also evident in technical translations. In translating advertising, translators are expected to take responsibility for the final form of an advertisement. Globalisation of the translation business sometimes means providing full marketing services in addition to translation and interpreting. Therefore, in the marketing of goods and services across cultural boundaries, an understanding of culture and semiotics that goes well beyond both language and design is involved. Translators need to understand the basics of marketing; they need to know the legal jurisdictions of their market; they must know how cultural differences affect marketing; they must be aware of constraints placed by the form and functions of the source text, and they must be able to interpret the visual elements which are of key importance in advertising. Going global successfully means taking control of the final product, researching the cultural and marketing aspects, and making sure the translation conforms to legal constraints. All this shows that the range of knowledge and skills needed by the profession of the translator is changing.

Introduction: Translation and the Translator

Recently *The European* (Smith, 1994) ran an article on an ad designed to sell Carlsberg beer. In the ad, a sheep dog walks into a room full of dancing sheep, strolls up to the bar, and asks for a Carlsberg beer. Brigitte Nielsen searches all over for a bottle opener, and when she does not find one, she opens the bottle between her ample breasts. The ad was designed in Denmark, for Denmark; it was sent over to the UK, where it was banned. Just one example of the many ways in which global marketing depends on knowledge of the target culture.

To what extent is the person who produces a target language version of an ad responsible for that knowledge? A translator could argue that translation is a discipline in its own right and that translators do not have the expertise or the legal responsibility to check on legislation, guard against copyright infringement, carry out market research, etc. in their home territory, let alone in foreign countries. In any case, so much of the work of global marketing bypasses translation, that a translator could almost be forgiven for thinking that this kind of work is best done by people in ad agencies. But only almost. Like it or not, the world is changing, and with it the boundaries of knowledge needed to exercise the profession. In terms of advancing our understanding of translation, it makes sense for there to be debate about the differences between translation and adaptation and an attempt to clarify the circumstances when one or the other is appropriate. But it is the marketplace more than an individual or professional philosophy that defines the responsibilities of the translator, and trying to restrict that role condemns translation to a service rather than a managerial role.

This paper considers a range of issues involved in the managing of international marketing, from the theoretical to the downright pragmatic, many of which fall into the category of being or having been someone else's responsibility. For example, design and layout considerations used to be the domain of graphic artists and they were often hidden away in print departments. Technology has changed all that. Today it is expected that translators produce camera-ready copy and that means taking responsibility for the final product. And as the visual element is key in promotional material, the marketing of goods and services across cultural boundaries involves an understanding of culture and semiotics that goes well beyond both language and design.

The globalisation of the translation business has led to the creation of language service companies which handle the localisation of computer products, media placement, and sometimes full marketing services in addition to translation and interpretation. Since there is an economic argument that encourages companies to standardise advertising during recessions, there can be an increased demand on translation services to provide translations for material which in fact needs to be adapted. Translators are implicitly expected to understand the requirements of different markets, and this means that translators need to understand the cultures towards which they are translating and in addition the basics of marketing.

Finally, there are the legal considerations: new markets mean new legal jurisdictions, and this often has consequences for translation.

Functionality versus Text Type

Going global means representing and marketing goods and services through-out the world. Advertising is of course the main vehicle for promotion, but promotion comes in all kinds of forms that may not look at all like ads. This distinction in terms of genres defines advertising as a text whose primary function is to move the audience to buy the product or service or be favourably disposed to the institution, party, company, etc. It therefore includes advocacy advertising, which often uses language which is quite different from product ads, as well as marketing and public relations material, which may not look like ads, but which often share some of the same features of language. In addition, certain kinds of promotional material — the labels on food products, for example — carry informative segments bound by different textual and regulative con-straints. In other words, cross-cultural promotion means a potential change in both form and content, and these changes can involve both text type and text functions.

The very act of promotion may not be acceptable in a given context in a given culture. Look at the area of public relations, for example. In modern hotels throughout the world there are booklets and directories of various kinds in the rooms. In North America these provide information, but they also have a public relations and hence a sales function. That explains why the description of the facilities and safety precautions are presented in terms of the services offered. Other cultures view this material in different ways. In Japan, for example, my five-star hotel provided a list of 'Rules of Conduct' which had the structure of a legal document. It began like this [the spelling errors have been reproduced]:

> In order to maintain the standards of the Hotel Concord Hamamatsu, our guests are requested to observe the following rules in accordance with the provisions Governing Accommodation Agreement Article 10.

The information about the availability of a safe for depositing valuables read like this:

Articles about valuables

(1) Deposit cash or valuables in the safety deposit box at the front desk.

(2) If cash or valuable which is not deposited is incurred, the hotel can not charge with it.

Guests who are familiar with western-style hotels expect a service orientation in this situation.

Again to illustrate how cultures view the functions of texts differently, someone has suggested that the bizarre use of English in Japanese marketing is related to the importance they give the visual aesthetic. In other words, combinations of words are selected for their graphic value rather than their meaning. This may explain why a name like Pocari Sweat , a very popular ion supply drink in Japan, is successful against all the intuitions of the native speaker.

Text and Context

Where does it go?

The media available and the contexts in which they operate mean that the way products are promoted potentially varies from country to country and from culture to culture (Benoît & Truchot, 1986: 14). To promote a product, you need to know what channels are available for that promotion. Take the simple example of give-aways. One of the ways our local merchants advertise is to give away free magnets. North Americans typically use their refrigerator doors as a message centre, so the magnets are a perfect way for a company to make sure its name and number are in view. That won't work in European households where fridges are built in behind cupboard doors or where the message centre has traditionally been a bulletin board placed near the only phone outlet (Norman, 1992).

I have known about electronic message boards in urban centres for a long time, but I have just learned that in parts of the US, ad agencies use liquid crystal displays mounted over the urinals in men's washrooms for promotions. On a recent visit to Amsterdam, I had a more personal experience of another marketing innovation available in several European cities: trendy restaurants and student haunts have started to carry racks of free postcards advertising everything from local markets to appeals for blood donors. It appears that there had been a swelling demand for advertising posters and someone thought up the postcard format as a response. And voilà, a whole new medium for promotion.

Even with traditional channels that are widespread, there may be restrictions on the kind of material that can be broadcast using that medium. Cuba's billboards promoting political causes have made it into coffee table art books. In Canada, billboard advertising is not used overtly for political campaign messages: the fortuitous 'Non, Merci!' on billboards close to the Quebec border in the province of Ontario just before the 1980 Quebec referendum on separation were attributed to the Ministry of Health and Welfare and their anti-alcohol campaign.

Text, context, and intertextuality

The twin influences of intertextuality and the relationship between text and context predispose a target audience to associate specific content with texts presented through a given medium. Ads can be more or less blatant and more or less integrated into their surroundings. In some countries advocacy-type advertising is unknown, and cultures differ as to whether they promote the corporate name or the product itself. In North America there has been a blurring of news and promotion; on TV we have the info-ad, in the print media, news stories written and paid for by corporate public relations departments. The fact that this material looks like the columns or programmes that surround it creates the illusion that the information is objective.

The relationship of promotional material to other material in a publication is crucial, and a translator responsible for buying space needs to look at the relationship between the translated text and the texts that surround it. An ad for gourmet food products placed opposite an appeal for funds for starving children is likely to be less effective than the same ad surrounded by advertising for exotic travel. The text of an ad for *Sabena Airlines* provides a classic example of the risks of interaction. The ad was repeated on billboards along the highway that thousands of French people take out of Paris the day vacations begin. The message was clever:

> Avec Sabena, vous y seriez déjà.
> [With Sabena, you'd be there already.]

But in France all kinds of walls are used for billboards, and one of the ads was placed on the brick wall around a cemetery.

Design and Layout Considerations

Many translators face the more mundane problems of placement in the form of multilingual packaging. Multilingual packaging is seen as key to establishing brand identification in a global market (Moriarity & Duncan, 1991: 327), and whereas advertising on television and billboards is generally done as original campaigns by advertising agencies, translators are most often responsible for the added languages on product packaging.

A few years ago one of our recent graduates came to me to show off her first translation for her new employer. It was a slogan for a cereal, and she was very proud of the way she had captured the word play of the original. But when the cereal boxes were printed, the slogan had been shortened, the word play was lost, and the whole was meaningless. Why did it happen? Because her version would not fit on the boxtop. Understanding space constraints is crucial when texts are going to be made available in several languages.

As more work is delivered electronically, it becomes even more important for translators to realise the changes that can potentially occur between the supplying of a translation and its appearance in printed form. Many translators have had the experience of handing in a text written in more than one language on a diskette only to have someone turn on an automatic hyphenating option designed for one language for the printed version, or had accents lost when text is scanned in electronically. Whenever a text goes through the hands of a typesetter or layout expert who is not familiar with the language, the translator needs to verify the final product. Graphic designers expect that there will be a specific relationship between text and white space, and they have been known to manipulate text for visual effect. A translator I know was horrified to see that the text he had translated for a museum exhibition was chopped up arbitrarily on the wall of the museum case so that each line in French was the length of the English line next to it and articles dangled helplessly in the air far from the nouns they were meant to introduce.

If the translator is responsible for producing the final copy, he or she needs to know the basics about typography. For this reason, an international advertising agency uses a set of images to show clients the effects of using such typographical devices as italics, block capitals, different fonts etc. on messages.

Even the insertion of pictures and illustrations that you supply can cause problems if the final results are not checked. A recent issue of Air Canada's newsletter for members of their mileage plan contained the following apology in English and in Japanese:

> The cover of the September/October issue of *Aeroplan World* featured three Japanese women wearing traditional kimonos. To our regret, when the photo was reversed to fit the layout, the fold on the kimonos was also inappropriately reversed. We extend our sincerest apologies to the Japanese community.

Reversing the way a kimono closes indicates that a death has occurred.

The fact that promotional material depends a lot on the visual, means that repairing translation errors can be costly. In Canada, the degree of tolerance for language errors in printed English and French is very low. A few years ago a student translated a few pages of marketing material for a car manufacturer into French for the Quebec market. The car dealers found several mistakes and refused to distribute the translated material. The company then sued the student, not to recover her fees, which were a couple of hundred dollars, but to recover the $40,000 cost of the four-colour printing of the brochures.

Getting the Goods…

Promotional material is an accessory to a product or a service. This means that the translator is constrained not only by the form and functions of the source text, but by the fact that there exists an object or a concept. An advertising agency may spend months analyzing a product before it decides on an approach; a translator may never get to see the object or speak to the providers of a service.

Now advertising sells by appealing to basic human emotions. You think you are buying a car? Marketing psychologists tell us that you are really buying power, sex, or love. To increase market share, promotional material creates distinctive images for products and companies (Barthes, 1957: 38–40). And both these marketing principles, the appeal to basic motivation and the positioning of a product in a market, are supported by conventional ideologies which in the western world include a tacit understanding that new is better, though paradoxically old-fashioned is purer, progress is good, and happiness can come out of a bottle.

That makes two problems so far: the fact that translation is a mediated response to an object or concept, and the fact that the motivating force behind the language of the source text is likely to be quite specific. Now the motivating force is generally carried by the more hidden messages, the connotative meaning (Barthes, 1964: 40–51). And connotations are notoriously culture-specific. How can the translator build in a different motivating factor if the legal, cultural, or marketing factors determine that the original is unacceptable? Without access to the product or information about the service, none.

Another problem that arises when there is no access to the product is the interpretation of metaphor. The instructions for the telecommunications system developed by IBM, the Rolm, are notoriously hard to interpret. Where I work we now have two French translations for the phone functions, one interpreting the English 'flash' in its connotative sense, 'eclair', the second, written by a translator who knew the frustrations of using the phone, 'garde', which is what the function is used for, commonly called 'hold' by other companies.

I have had the dubious pleasure of experiencing this challenge myself while translating a marketing brochure for a pressure cooker from French to English. Part of the pressure cooker was referred to with the metaphor 'clip'. There was a 'clip vert' and a 'clip rouge' i.e. a red and a green 'clip' to indicate what they called cooking speeds. The literal translation of 'clip' is 'broach', the piece of ladies' jewellery, which is no help at all. No access to the product, no access to a picture of the product, no access to a qualified person as the contract came through an ad agency, and not to the manufacturer.

The Notion of Iconicity

The source text is written with the knowledge of the product or service in mind. And just as a text can interact with the physical context and with the texts with which it is surrounded, a text bears a relationship to them and to the visual and graphic elements associated with the marketing process. Borrowing a term from Peirce (Fiske, 1982: 51), we can describe these relationships in terms of the degree of iconicity, meaning the extent to which the relationships in which they stand are based on a non-arbitrary similarity. Although these kinds of relationships are not restricted to any specific kind of text, the difficulties that they pose for translation are particularly frequent in advertising, marketing, and public relations material.

Among the more exotic instances of relationships are the cases where the packaging of an item is deliberately designed to echo the name: L'eggs pantyhose, for example, is sold in egg-like containers. Typically the translation difficulty is lexical, and it is hard to compensate for the loss of relatedness. Manipulation of the source language to pretend that it is a reflection of a foreign language is another difficulty as different cultures hold very different views about other cultures and the interpretation of what is politically correct. To announce a sale of office furniture, a copywriter in Toronto established an iconic link between the name of the store, Nienkämper, and the text. The Germanicisation of the English acts as a separate sign to convey the connotation of imported and European:

> Der maeker of der verlds fineist leäther kredenzan und chairen inviitens u tu der annualen furniker einventory salen (from *The Globe and Mail*, February 28, 1991).

A more obvious kind of relationship is the use of pictures and illustrations to convey the qualities that are being attributed to the product. As with all semiotic readings, the relationships can be iconic, symbolic, or indexical. An iconic representation is one where the graphics show the product: the resemblance is based on identity. A symbolic representation shows the qualities that are to be associated with the product, while an indexical relationship indicates the personal qualities that can be attributed to the owner of the product through a process of logical deduction, for example the wealth and status necessary to acquire the product.

An example of this is a car ad which shows an iconic representation of a moving car. The streaks in the graphics not only represent movement, they symbolise speed and power. This connotation of power is reflected in the text through the use of words like 'knockout'. Even if the slogan 'technical knockout' poses problems in a different language, the selling feature is clear.

One of the jobs of the translator working with this kind of material is to ensure that there is this consistency, that the selling motivation is made clear through a harmonising of the connotations with the information denoted in the text and images. An iconic representation of a product has both a plus and a down side: it provides a certain amount of factual information, but that information is also available to the reader. An example of what happens when the translator works only on the level of language comes from an ad for French lingerie that appeared in the *New York Times*. The product, a matching set of underwear, was see-through, made of lace, relatively skimpy. The model has struck a seductive pose, her shirt flying loose and her fingers combing through her hair. The connotative reinforced the sexy image of the product. The words in the slogan, however, 'LEJABY comfortable ... like no other bra in the world', conveyed a different impression from the image.

The way in which the reader or viewer identifies with the people portrayed in an ad is also a potential marketing problem. Is the picture a representation of who the readers or viewers perceive themselves to be, someone they can identify with, or someone with symbolic value, a supermodel who epitomises sex, beauty, power... In some cultures the exotic sells, in others a lack of identification can mean a lack of trust. It appears that successful ads in Lebanon show men dressed conservatively, which is consistent with the behaviour of the readers and viewers of the ads, but that a blond woman adds interest (Kaynak, 1989: 135). Taboos are clearly out: a firm tried to sell refrigerators in the Middle East with a picture of its appliance filled with food — including a large ham. And as we will discuss further on when we turn to cultural issues, western symbolic and indexical values clearly differ from those of the east: a westerner designed an ad for Ivory Soap for use in China. It showed a family working in the rice paddies and coming back dirty. In China, the image of dirtiness is insulting (Xu Bai Y, 1990: 86). The article that mentioned this failure suggested that the best ad that had been done for this product was the one that said 'Ivory — the soap that floats'. An ad for which the visuals would have to be totally different.

When an illustration has a non-iconic relationship with the product, the translator's job can be more difficult. For example, another car ad carries an arresting photo of adorable forest creatures all in a row. Here, too, there is a mirroring of the photo in the language as the text personifies the animals: 'The fawn thanks you', it begins. But the appropriate reading of the photo depends on culture. These animals are familiar to North Americans; what is unfamiliar is the way in which they have been photographed, i.e. in a line-up. This artificial ordering symbolises control, the control that is the selling feature of this particular model. The ad plays on the sensibilities of readers who have been moved by the sight of these familiar animals dead by the side of the road. But what about a readership which has never seen some of these animals? With an iconic illustration of a product, the translator can search for other features to highlight. With a non-iconic illustration, how does the translator find the information in order to re-orient the text?

It is paradoxical, but the solution to global marketing is not necessarily to rely more on visuals. It is well-known in advertising that the visuals are extremely important in reaching a niche market. Place an ad in an English pub, and the reader or viewer gets an enormous amount of information about the sexual orientation, the class and education level of the people in the scene. Even the non-iconic visual ads that deliver style rather than narrative, the ads that step out of the semiotic framework centred on the reader and his or her motivations to grab attention for the brand name, face cultural values. Owners of Benetton franchises in Germany, for example, have blamed the controversial Benetton ads for their poor sales.

To Market, to Market...

Types of markets

Going global means understanding the difference between writing for a market and creating one. There are two kinds of ads: those designed to introduce a product or service and those designed to take business away from the competition. If the original choice of language was designed for a market in which there are competitors and the target text is destined for virgin territory, the campaign will likely fail. First you have to create a need — it is a breakfast cereal, it is a treat for your family, it will save you hours in the kitchen, it will impress your neighbours. You drink it, spread it on toast, wear it after skiing.

Explaining what a product is may also mean expanding on its use. It is not obvious that you need to pour milk on breakfast cereal, and because it was never explained to them, the French and Scandinavians treat cereal as a snack food (Moriarity & Duncan, 1991: 326; Circus, 1987: 64).

Creating a market for a product is not obvious. When Perrier water was first introduced in North America, the selling feature was health. This tied in with the general marketing of bottled waters in France that plays on a preoccupation with digestion. We all know what happened when the new campaign was launched to focus on the sophistication of drinking water in places where people traditionally drink alcohol. The concept of a special sports drink that restores your ion balance after a workout seems to have had limited success in North America, where Gatorade is still on the shelves, but remarkable results in Japan where there is a range of ion supply drinks.

What is the motivating factor in the source text? Is it appropriate for the target market? There is no point writing about the labour-saving appeal of a product if the advertising is going to a nation of cheap human labour. What Scandinavians care most about shampoo is that it will help them feel clean. Japanese women would like their hair to hold a curl, and if they shampoo their hair often, it is linked to their desire to look different.

You cannot write about the value of staying young in cultures that revere old age, and you cannot even assume that having white teeth is a plus because of the number of countries where if you have money you chew betel nuts — which stain your teeth brown.

Positioning new products globally is easier than repositioning existing products. Established brands may have different images and different positioning strategies. Horlicks is sold as a night-time drink that helps you get to sleep in Britain; in Thailand it is seen as an energy-giving morning drink. A bicycle is a luxury sports item in North America but a means of transport in many parts of the world. The positioning and pricing strategies of Godiva chocolates are different in France and the US compared to Belgium.

To isolate the marketing strategy for translation it helps to view a text as a directed reading of the visuals. Will the target population identify with the representation of the user of the product? Take the example of exporting cream rinse. The English blurb recommends these products for use with over-processed hair. The translator has the choice of providing this information in another language or, in a market where women prize straight hair, considering another marketing strategy that suggests that cream rinse helps relax curls. Even in cultures that are very close there is a need to be aware of cultural differences that affect marketing. In the US and English Canada, for example, soup is viewed and marketed as a food for children. In French Canada, soup is accepted as a family meal, and there are usually separate campaigns for that reason.

Cultural perspectives

I have already labelled some of the conventional ideologies used to position a company or a product in a market as 'western'. But before we look at the differences between eastern and western values, it is obvious that there are cultural differences among nations in the west. Attitudes to children is one area that causes problems for multinational companies. The typical American commercial for breakfast cereals is centred on the child who interacts with a parent or an animated character. The child initiates discussion. In many cultures this is not acceptable. The child-centred approach works in North America because children have buying power, either directly or through their ability to whine their way to their products of choice. If you compare print advertising directed to products or services intended for children in North America and in France, you see a clear difference in theme. The French approach is that the advertiser has the expertise, and the parent has the authority. In North America the underlying motivation is a desire to see one's child happy and there may be an overt appeal to feelings of guilt and inadequacy on the part of the parents.

While in some cultures guilt and inadequacy are used to sell, in others they can interfere with sales. It would not be a good idea to advertise a one-step floor wax in Germany as a way of eliminating the need to scrub the floor. Self-image is simply too invested in the activity (Kaynak, 1989: 134). In this regard it is useful to consider the difference that advertising research makes between high-involvement ads and low-involvement ads. In North America, for example, toothpaste ads directed to families are high involvement as mothers take their role in teaching their children to brush their teeth very seriously.

Two general kinds of distinctions have been made between types of cultures as far as advertising is concerned. The first is the tendency to prefer either style and visuals — like France and Japan — to text and argumentation, as in North America (Kaynak, 1989: 134). The second is the distinction referred to as western versus eastern based on communication patterns and decision-behaviour values (Frith & Frith, 1990: 69–70). Where directness and coming to the point are valued in the west, euphemism and politeness are seen as appropriate in the east. It is considered very rude in many eastern cultures to mention price. The individualism of the west contrasts with a respect for authority and identity with a group in the east. And the western gung-ho attitude that effort and hard work lead to success is opposed to some eastern spiritual and religious notions of resignation and fate. A word of warning though: the east is by no means a unified market. To sell to the Japanese, it is effective to emphasise style and glamour; to sell to the Chinese, what works is product durability and performance.

Many cultures have taboos about sex and alcohol that make their way into legislation, but there are many cultural norms that are not written down that need to be taken into account. Ads for breath fresheners use couples in the western world; in Thailand it is considered improper for such things to be discussed between men and women.

It is also crucial to understand the symbolic weight of objects. A perfume campaign in Latin America failed because it emphasised the scent of fresh camellias. Camellias are the flower most often associated with funerals in Latin America (Slater, 1984).

Different cultures are also sensitised to different issues of political correctness. It is clear that since the early 1970s the portrayal of women and of minorities in advertising and more recently the elderly has been more discussed in the U.S. than in the European Union (Cutler & Rajshekh, 1992: 73).

The translator/advertiser also needs to be aware of attitudes towards the culture of origin of the product. These perceptions may be very complex: in some markets it works to identify a product as imported, for example clothes marked 'Made in USA' sell well in Japan. In others, it is a bad thing, as in the case of American cars for sale in Japan.

Culture versus subculture

There are two reasons why the role of culture in marketing may be difficult to predict. The first is the fact that a country may not be a unified market. China is a case in point, with a variety of different ethnic groups spread over a huge territory. The second reason is the growing significance of global communication which blurs national differences. Age and lifestyle may be more important than national culture. Thanks to satellite TV, adolescents the world over have more in common with their peers in other countries in terms of their tastes than with other age groups from the same culture (Kaynak, 1989: 132–3). Another group that forms a common market across cultures is the business traveller.

Language issues

Wordplay, cultural and literary allusions, terms that translate differently for different countries in the case of wide distribution, these are all familiar problems. The classic example of untranslatable wordplay is the ad for the French aperitif Dubonnet that used to be painted on the walls of the Paris subway years ago. As the cars went by, riders would see just part of the word:

Dubo ... Dubon ... Dubonnet

In French, each part has meaning, in English, none.

The more countries a text is meant for, the greater the potential for dialect differences that affect the choice of terms, and even of script. A common example of the problem comes from translating recipes into English where there is the need to choose between 'cookie' and 'biscuit', 'castor sugar' and 'sugar'. Another classic problem is the choice of unsuitable names in the source language as with the Chevy 'Nova' which promises not to go in Spanish. And wherever a product is marketed, there is a chance that the name will be associated with an existing product in the target country. 'Durex' is the name for a condom in Britain. In Australia, it is an adhesive tape.

The fact that advertising is regulated by all kinds of legislation means that a translator sometimes has to beware of dictionaries. In Quebec, for example, the most common term for 'infant formula' is 'lait maternisé'. But companies are not allowed to use it on their products because the Food and Drug Act specifies that the term has to be 'préparation pour nourrissons', which no speaker actually uses.

Another problem on the level of language is that translators are human, and like other readers, they can be fooled by weasel words, those little expressions that seem to promise good things but mean nothing. A product may say that it will help you lose weight, but that is not a guarantee you will lose weight. The term 'warehouse price' is easily misinterpreted as meaning 'wholesale price' when it is nothing of the kind.

Just as translators need to be aware of a culture's tolerance for directness, they need to become aware of the elements of copywriting to produce effective promotional copy. You don't remind people of the negative; you write, 'to stay slim ...', not 'if you're fat ...'.

Trademarks

The choice of trademark is a special case of language use. There are laws governing both the registration and in some cases the use of trademark. A law recently passed in France regulating the use of foreign language in advertising has affected trademarks as well as the copy of ads. But even where there is no legislation, the same issues of symbolic value apply as with text. In China, the elephant brings luck. 'White Elephant' batteries did not do well in the west (Xu Bai Yi, 1990: 85). Neither did another of the Chinese exports, 'Pansy' brand men's underwear (*Business International*, 1987: 53).

An Illustration of the Issues: The Case of Cointreau

A good example of translation issues in global marketing can be found in the recent advertising for the liqueur Cointreau. A German magazine played on the prestige of the French name with a full-page picture of a sophisticated woman and, underneath, the line, 'Voulez-vous Cointreau avec moi?'. The Canadian market experienced two kinds of ads. Articles about the marketing of Cointreau that appeared about the time of the ad campaign made it clear the company was trying to reposition the product in order to increase sales. The idea was to encourage people to order and serve Cointreau as a cocktail as well as a liqueur. The first campaign that ran in magazines used a translation for the English. The ad as it appeared in French depended on a strong visual to attract the reader's attention, then tied it in to the product: a large square orange was used to mirror the square bottle that holds the orange liqueur. This iconicity was carried over in the original French text through the metaphoric reference, 'L'Orange carrée [the square orange] se déguste nature, avec glaçons ou en cocktail' and through the denotation of the morpheme 'carré', meaning square, in the slogan 'Carrément Cointreau'.

The English translation treated all the information in the source text as equally valuable. To compensate for the lost references to squareness in the French wordplay, the translator added the notion of global sales:

The distinctive orange taste in the distinctive cubic bottle is enjoyed throughout the four corners of the world — straight, on the rocks, with a spritz, or in cocktails.

The word 'cubic' and the repetition of 'distinctive' also seem to be an attempt at compensation. The text is lengthened, and it is less obvious that the intention of the advertisement was to change Cointreau's image. The iconicity has a purely stylistic function rather than supporting the repositioning of the message that Cointreau can be served before as well as after a meal.

A few months after these ads were published, a quite different approach to the same product appeared in an urban newspaper read by the target market, young adults. The illustration showed a pretty young woman in a black leather jacket with unzipped zippers running up the sleeves. One eye drooped shut, and she supported her head in her hands as though she had a hangover. Why a hangover? Because it implies that this is a drink that is strong, that you can get drunk on. The text supported this image with the highlighted words 'the blast' and the lines, 'bittersweet orange, with the art of Opalescence. Cointreau on Ice the original premium imported spirit from France.' 'Premium' brings to mind the collocation premium beer, 'spirit', hard liquor. In the right-hand corner of the ad, under the name from the Cointreau label, are the words 'on ice' and on the page over the model's picture are the single words 'ice', 'and' 'heat', and 'rock'. The non-narrative use of words, the graphics, the model's leather motorcycle jacket underscore the hardness of the image.

Who has the power to create a different promotional strategy? It depends on the country and the client. Certainly in Canada the current language policy encourages the creation of parallel texts, as in the example of a company called *Participaction* that promotes a healthy lifestyle. The photos in the French and English versions can be different, the text can be different, and the connotative values can be different. In one campaign, the French and English used three horizontal photos with simple labels. The French showed a bicycle, underneath it dried pasta and vegetables, and under that a picture of a smiling man. The text read: BONNE BÉCANE, BONNE RECETTE, BONNE FORME, which can be glossed as 'Good bike, good recipe, good health'. The English text showed a pair of shoes, underneath it some slices of fruit, and under that a female athlete known locally where the ad was placed. The text read: PATTI HABIB'S SNEAKERS, PATTI HABIB'S 'POWER' SNACK, PATTI HABIB. In both versions food symbolises health, but the French reference to recipes plays on the status aspect of food for the French while the 'Power Snack' in the English ad plays on the collocation 'power breakfast' and the goal of business success.

Legislation

Stepping into different cultures means crossing national boundaries, and that means entering different legislative jurisdictions. Checking on whether a name has been registered in a particular jurisdiction or whether there are regulations that would prohibit the showing of particular material is so complex that it is impossible to make a complete list of directives and authorities. The table that has been provided is only an indication of the major areas of legislation.

In the case of a federated state, there may be both local and national laws. In Europe, in addition to EU Directives on trade practices and advertising, member states to a large extent have the right to pass more restrictive legislation in these areas provided that it is not protectionist, i.e. it must apply equally to domestic production and to products imported from other members of the EU. The standardisation of regulations in the EU is the subject of huge debate in a number of very specific areas. Two of these are the harmonisation of definitions of misleading advertising and unfair advertising. The Union is also dealing with the problem of satellites that can beam a programme with advertising allowed in one country into another one where the laws are more restrictive. A political will to carry out a social policy can also impact on the language used in marketing: the European Commission recently discussed the possibility of regulating the reference to speed and power to promote car sales as a way of reducing traffic fatalities. With each change in presidency of the Union come new agendas. Spain, for example, has already promised to look into sexism in ads when it takes over next year (Smith, 1994).

Table 1 A sampling of the major areas in which legislation affects advertising (this list is based in part on information from Boddewyn, 1981: 5–13)

Issue	Country or Organization
Audience Protection:	
Advertising to children;	Canada, Scandinavia, US
Infant formula promotion;	World Health Organization, UNICEF
Privacy protection	
Health and Safety Issues:	
Labelling on food products and	EU, US, Canada
language in food and drug ads	
Consumer Protection:	
Class Action suits allowed by	
consumer associations:	EU, US
Corrective ads:	EU, US
Reversal of burden of proof on	
the advertiser:	EU, Scandinavia, US
Labour Protection:	
Use of child actors:	Austria
Cultural and Language Issues:	
Sexism:	Canada, Netherlands, India, Scandinavia, UK, US
Feminine hygiene ads:	Canada
Use of foreign language in ads:	France, Mexico, Province of Quebec
Use of foreign materials, themes, illustrations:	Korea, Muslim countries, Peru, Philippines, Malaysia
Market Protection:	
Comparison advertising:	EU, France, US, Philippines
Trans-border data flow:	EU, Norway, US

Many laws affect the naming of products. Names may be registered, and it is a good idea to check in all the jurisdictions affected to see whether a name has already been claimed before it goes on expensive packaging. The question of whether a source language trademark gets retained, combined with, or replaced by a target language trademark is a marketing issue. Any products related to food or health may be subject to labelling laws which require the inclusion of particular kinds of information and which may prohibit or restrict the use of particular terms. Words like 'natural', for example, are strictly regulated. And then there are the language watchdogs like the Office de la langue française in Quebec which fixes terms where people might be tempted to adopt *anglicismes*.

Laws can also oblige you to say more than you intended. The Malaysian Advertising Code states that 'In addition to the commercial message, all advertisements must also contain a second message relating to cleanliness, healthy living, discipline or industrious attitude.' (Frith & Frith, 1990: 68).

Conclusion

In promotional material, the success of a translation is a function of the relationships the text has with its context, the visuals accompanying it, and the preparation of the market. Going global successfully means taking control of the final product, researching the cultural and marketing aspects, and making sure the translation conforms to the legal constraints.

References

Barthes, R. (1964) Rhétorique de l'image. *Communications* 4, 40–51.

— (1957) Saponides et détergents. *Mythologies*. Paris: Éditions du Seuil.

Benoît, P. and Truchot, D. (1986) *Affiches de Pub 1983/85*. Paris: Chêne.

Boddewyn, J.J. (1981) The global spread of advertising regulations. *MSU Business Topics*, Spring, 5–13.

Business International Asia/Pacific Ltd. (1987) *Advertising Strategies for China: Markets, Media and Measurement*. Hong Kong, 50–3.

Circus, P. (1987) Trademarks: Marketing tool or legal minefield? *Trademark World*, April 1987.

Cutler, B.D. and Rajshekh, G. (1992) A cross-cultural analysis of the visual components of print advertising: The United States and the European Community. *Journal of Advertising Research*, January/February.

Fiske, J. (1982) *Introduction to Communication Studies*. London/New York: Methuen.

Frith, K.T. and Frith, M. (1990) Western advertising and Eastern culture: The confrontation in Southeast Asia. *Current Issues in Research in Advertising* 12 (1 & 2).

Kaynak, E. (1989) *The Management of International Advertising: A Handbook and Guide for Professionals*. USA: Quorum Books.

Moriarity, S. and Duncan, T. (1991) Global advertising: Issues and practices. *Current Issues in Research in Advertising* 13 (1 & 2), 327.

Norman, D.A. (1992) *Turn Signals are the Facial Expressions of Automobiles* (pp. 48–58). Reading, MA/New York: Addison-Wesley.

Slater, J.R. (1984) The hazards of cross-cultural advertising. *Business America*, April 2.

Smith, S. (1994) Advertising the sex factor. In *The European*, October 7–13.

Xu, B.Y. (1990) *Marketing to China: One Billion New Customers*. Illinois: NTC Business Books.

Further reading

Aeroplan World 1995 2 (1), January/February.

Alden, D.L., Hoyer, W.D. and Lee, C. (1993) Identifying global and culture-specific dimensions of humor in advertising: A multinational analysis. *Journal of Marketing* 57, 64–75.

Biswas, A., Olsen, J.E. and Carlet, V. (1992) A comparison of print advertisements from the United States and France. *Journal of Advertising* 21 (4), December.

Caples, J. (1975) *Tested Advertising Methods*. Toronto: Prentice-Hall.

Carrier, M. (1979) La femme imaginaire de la publicité. *Protégez-vous*, September 1979.

Commission of the European Communities (1990) *Consumer Policy in the Single Market*. Luxembourg: Office for Official Publications of the European Communities.

Crumley, B. (1994) France's restrictive new laws create headaches for ad industry. *Advertising Age*, 4 July 1994.

Di Sardi, N. (1991) Reaching a unique market: It takes more than translation to make ethnic ads work. *Marketing*, June 17.

Galliot, M. (1955) *Essai sur la Langue de la Réclame Contemporaine*. Toulouse: Edouard Privat.

Graham, J.L., Kamins, M.A. and Oetomo, D.S. (1993) Content analysis of German and Japanese advertising in print media from Indonesia, Spain, and the United States. *Journal of Advertising* 22 (2), June.

Groves, P. (1991) *Copyright and Design Laws: A Question of Balance*. London: Graham and Trotman.

Haight, A. (1993) Car ads draw scrutiny: European commission to discourage speed, power claims. *Advertising Age International*, May 17.

Hallenstein, D. (1995) Images on Fire with Moral Ideas. *The European Magazine*, February 3–9.

Harrington, K. (ed.) (1975) *Principles and Practices of Classified Advertising*. Milwaukee: Assoc. of Newspaper Classified Advertising Managers, Inc. 89–98.

Hepner, H. (1969) *AdvertisingCreative Communication with Consumers* (3rd edn). New York: McGraw-Hill.

Kincaid, L.D. (1987) *Communication Theory: Eastern and Western Perspectives*. California: Academic Press.

Leballeaux, P. (1976) *La Publicité Directe*. Paris: Les Editions d'Organisation.

Leech, G.N. (1966) *English in Advertising*. London: Longman.

McKay, B. (1992) Xerox fights trademark battle. *Advertising Age International*, April 27.

Meta (1972) *Numéro Spécial sur la Publicité* 17, 1 March.

Miracle, G.E. (1988) An empirical study of the usefulness of the back-translation technique for international advertising messages in print media. *Proceedings of the 1988 Conference of the American Academy of Advertising*.

— (1990) The advertising environment, advertising law, and the standardization of international advertising: The case of Japan and the USA. *Proceedings of the 1990 Conference of the Academy of American Advertising*.

Miracle, G.E. *et al.* (1989) Teaching International Advertising. *Proceedings of the 1989 Conference of the American Academy of Advertising*.

Noble, V. (1970) *The Effective Echo. A Dictionary of Advertising Slogans*. New York: Special Library Associations.

Ogilvy, D. (1962) *Confessions of an Advertising Man*. New York: Atheneum.

Pasadeos, Y. (1991) Advertising information as a societal variable: factual cues in U.S., German and Greek magazine advertisements. *Proceedings of the 1991 Conference of the American Academy of Advertising*.

Plummer, J.T. (1986) The role of copy research in multinational advertising. *Journal of Advertising Research*, Oct–Nov.

Pollay, R.W. (1990) Normative beliefs about advertising: An exploratory study of Chinese consumers. Paper presented at Canada–China International Management Conference Xi'an, China, 1990. *Research Papers in International Business, Trade & Finance*, Faculty of Commerce and Business Administration, University of British Colombia.

Pritchard, B. (1989) Clearing the confusion of trademark violations. *Marketing* 94/7 October 16.

Ricks, D.A. (1983) *Big Business Blunders. Mistakes in Multinational Marketing*. Homewood, IL: Dow Jones-Irwin.

Rosenberg, J. (1991) *The New Europe. A–Z Compendium on the European Community*. Washington, DC: Bureau of National Affairs Inc.

Short, D. (1995) BBC joins advertising world. *The European*, February 3–9.

Stone, B. (1979) *Successful Direct Marketing Methods*. Chicago: Crain Books.

Subramanian, D. (1991) Comparative ads spark debate. *Marketing*, February 11.

Tatilon, C. (1978) Traduire la parole publicitaire. *La Linguistique* 14 (1) 75–87.

The Chartered Institute of Patent Agents (1990) *CIPA Handbook to the Patents Act* (3rd edn). London: Sweet & Maxwell.

The Economist 1990, Single Marketing, March 24.

Woodroffe, G. (ed.) (1984) *Consumer Law in the EEC*. London: Sweet & Maxwell.

DEBATE

Cultural Taboos in Translating Advertising

Mona Baker (UMIST/University of Middlesex): I would like to comment on one of the examples you have shown, the advertisement for a slimming product, which shows part of a body which can easily be recognised as that of a young, slim woman. Of course, cultural differences are highly relevant here. The whole idea of females wanting to lose weight, especially to this extent, wouldn't appeal to an Arab market at all, where it's not particularly pleasant to be very slim — some people think the opposite in fact. So from this angle, the angle of losing weight, this product wouldn't have a market.

Said Faiq (University of Salford): But I think things are changing. In your paper, Candace, you said that it would be inappropriate to name price in an ad in the Arab world. Although this was the case in that culture, things have changed a lot and now people are naming prices in their ads, for instance in car ads. And I have indeed seen adverts on Egyptian television which appeal to people wanting healthy bodies.

Mona Baker: But these were appealing to health — and it's all relative. If you were even allowed to put an ad like this in the paper, the woman would look anorexic enough as it is. Also, this would appeal to a particular age group and a particular class, because in the Arab world if you're a professional woman you have to be of a certain age and a certain build to be taken seriously. Being young and slim does not earn you respectability. So the company would have to create a market for this product by trying to change people's concepts and perceptions. But the market would not be ready-made as it is, for example, in France.

Said Faiq: You should be wary about these over-generalisations. Putting advertising aside, we should really be cautious when making statements about individual cultures, particularly these days. The statistics in the paper date back to 1981 where Candace says that something would apply to certain countries but not to Arab cultures. I don't think we can be so sure about this any more. Things have changed a lot in 14 years.

Mona Baker: But you can't do without generalisation in academic research. We all know it's dangerous, but if you're not going to generalise to a certain extent, there's no point in the exercise at all.

Said Faiq: But you cannot see the Arab world as a whole. For example, a charity which was advertising in the Middle East — in Saudi Arabia and the United Arab Emirates — used two different advertising texts for both countries. In fact, the text used in the United Arab Emirates could have been used in Britain, whereas the text for Saudi Arabia was designed in a very different way, although these two countries are neighbours.

Helen Kelly-Holmes (Aston University): The graphic in the ad and the idea of

72

weight-losing also make the ad self-selecting. It is only going to attract women who have a certain self-image or an ideal and are interested in losing weight to achieve this. By using such a graphic, the advertiser alienates other women and men who may not conform to this image but who may actually have a need for the product.

Candace Séguinot: This is really key for me, because this is a product, like many others, which could be of use to older people and yet no-one is willing to target that market, as it's not very glamorous.

Anthony Mathews (Birkbeck College UL): Another problem with this ad is that it is for a product which aids the digestive process, something which is embarrassing for most English people. So you would have to allow for this by, for example, using 'tummy' rather than 'stomach' in the translation. I think this would work better in an English context.

Helen Kelly-Holmes: Isn't that a bit childish?

Anthony Mathews: But there's a whole vocabulary of infantilism, I suppose I'd call it, attached to medical terms in English. Would this also apply in North America?

Candace Séguinot: I think when you're dealing with taboos, the way in which you refer to them is really quite specific and I'm not sure that you would refer to this area of the body at all in North America. I personally would refer to a feeling of heaviness.

Anthony Mathews: Or you could get around this taboo by referring to the problem in this infantile way. Then you're going into the semi-jocular which would be the way it would be advertised in this country.

Rachel Brough (University of Surrey): That, however, would clash with the picture that shows a slim body of a young woman, and this appeals to a sophisticated market.

Paul Kußmaul (Germersheim University): I think the concept of sub-cultures is also interesting here. There may be a subculture or subcultures within a culture which are interested in this product.

Helen Kelly-Holmes: I agree with this. It's very important not to be hooked on national culture and instead to look more at lifestyle culture, which can be shared by groups in different countries.

Beverly Adab (Aston University): This is the essence of global advertising — a cross-cultural appeal to the universals of a given lifestyle.

Redefining the Role of the Translator

Candace Séguinot: The concept of lifestyle and group cultures is important for technical translation, with knowledge and cultural values being shared by, for example, professional groups in various cultures. The translator who just looks to the fact that this particular ad is addressed to the woman in the picture can't take on the extra role, which is to sit back and say: this is a really good product, I wonder whether there's a place for it and make a suggestion to the manufacturer. This is not the way translation is currently done — unless someone owns a company which also does advertising and marketing.

Margaret Rogers (University of Surrey): Isn't the really interesting thing about this the issue of where the translator's competence starts and finishes and where the marketing competence starts and finishes. There are some things which would be immediately obvious to someone who knows another culture and language, but then there are some things that may not be quite so obvious because the translator does not have the expertise in marketing. What interests me is where these two things overlap or where they divide.

Christina Schäffner (Aston University): This is getting to the heart of the matter, and this was one of Candace's points in her paper. Do translators just get the text with no other information or do they work in-house and have access to the product and expertise? This is obviously relevant for the final form of the translation product.

Kirsten Malmkjaer (Cambridge University): The problem here is how exactly to define the role of the translator. Are we talking about translation or about deconstructing the advertising, which is what I think we're talking about — deconstructing the message and then recreating it as something very different for a different culture.

Margaret Rogers: From which model of translation are we working and arguing? Surely not from a purely linguistic model, since there's another model and another way of working. I once went to a very interesting talk given by someone who runs what he calls a multilingual copywriting service. He started out wanting to earn his living translating advertisements, but he soon decided that he couldn't and now he runs this type of business. In this model, a separate marketing strategy is created for each country and then copywriters in those countries are employed to write the ads and he oversees and coordinates the whole process.

Kirsten Malmkjaer: I think the most important thing in translating advertising is to preserve the perlocutionary effect — after all that is what advertising is about. If you're going to sell the product by appealing to the clients, that's a perlocutionary effect and we have to keep that in mind when we talk about translating ads, and this takes us into pragmatics.

Heike Perry (Aston University): In effect, we seem to be coming to the conclusion that we can't translate an advert. If your idea of translation is taking a text and transforming it into another language, then, of course, you can't translate it. With advertising, what you maybe need to do is say this is the concept, the idea, now go and write the text.

Christina Schäffner: This is what Brian Harris called 'co-writing', a Canadian practice where an English and French writer are each told the purpose of the text and the main ideas, and then the two texts are produced in parallel, but independent of each other.

Legal Problems

Candace Séguinot: In most consumer goods companies there is a team. For example, in Nestlé there's a whole team working on translation — made up not just of translators. There is also a medical doctor who handles the scientific component, and some translators who deal with specific parts of the world and some who have various product specialisms. But what is key for them in their jobs is that they know the legislation. They are told not just to rely on dictionaries but to go and find out about the relevant legislation, because sometimes laws have been translated by people who do not have adequate legal knowledge.

Beverly Adab: But legislation only regulates the form of the message, not the constellation of cultural or subcultural values for which it is a vehicle.

Peter Newmark (University of Surrey): The question of where the work of the translator stops and that of the marketing expert begins really depends on how independent the translator is. If the translator has his/her own agency, then s/he can say how much they're going to do.

Candace Séguinot: What I've noticed is that people who own agencies can decide on what they advertise their agency as doing, and that's where it starts. Through localisation, agencies can offer more than translation — this is what happened when they started to offer typesetting services.

Peter Newmark: What is your definition of localisation here? Is it relating to a specific market?

Candace Séguinot: I'm thinking here of computer products. For example, when a company designs a piece of software and exports it to a country with another language, localisation means translating and adapting that product so that people in the country can work in their national language with that product — changing keyboards, for example, would be one of the services.

Geoffrey Samuelsson-Brown (Aardvark Translation Services): On the subject of localisation, the way we work is to send — wherever possible — the translation to the company's subsidiary in the country where the language is spoken. They can then localise the text in terms of legislation, language, buzz words and so on. But, as you said, you can define localisation differently depending on whether you mean computer software or other products.

Candace Séguinot: Let's take the example of pharmaceuticals. In North America you have to be careful about something which indicates a symptom. There's generally a formulation in the text like — if pain continues, see a doctor. So, if you were translating the ad for a North American audience, you would have to include this. The translator needs to be aware of these differences of liability in different countries.

Beverly Adab: But the translator could construct the translation to avoid the ambiguity so as not to incur this liability. If the company is not a multinational, they wouldn't be producing ads with a view to an international market. Rather they'd be targeting a specific market. Also, the awareness of the text type convention for a given type in a given market will be a pre-requisite for the task.

Candace Séguinot: I don't know if this is the case. This pharmaceutical company I was referring to is working within Europe.

Beverly Adab: The problem with pharmaceuticals though is that whatever you produce in your own country cannot necessarily be exported to another country. So there is a tendency to reproduce advertising for specific products based on their use and attractiveness for that particular country, that is the source culture, without due reference to the conceptual framework (product licensing) and marketing conventions of a target culture.

Candace Séguinot: A lot of pharmaceutical companies in Canada have in-house translators to translate their advertising.

Beverly Adab: Yes, but that's because of the Canadian situation. It's still the same country. The trans-European problem is that licensing is different in different countries for a given product, so that a drug used to treat cancer in one country cannot necessarily be prescribed for similar use in another country, but may be used to treat a different condition.

Candace Séguinot: But in Canada there's also a different licensing system in the different states, and I've actually seen advertising for the French market which is different.

Beverly Adab: Different in what way — in the illness to be treated or in the marketing approach? And do they not come under the same national rules for product licensing?

Candace Séguinot: Yes and no! There's actually been a book written about how to win court cases based on the differences between English and French translations of laws. It's not only the differences in language but also in the legal system. There's the French translation of the English common law and there's the Napoleonic Code in Quebec and there can be English versions of that.

Carmen Arnaiz (University of the West of England): But saying that the translator should know all about related legislation in each country is a bit much.

Candace Séguinot: But it's absolutely necessary in Canada.

Training and Educational Implications

Mona Baker: What are the implications of all this for training translators to do this kind of work? If you set up a course which teaches people to do this kind of technical translation and also teaches them how to research the laws of different countries, do you think there would be a big enough market for such specialised staff? So, what is the demand in the market and how do you train people to satisfy this demand?

Candace Séguinot: I want to teach people skills rather than labelling, so that when they come out at the end wanting to be translators and finding there are no jobs, they don't feel suicidal. What we try to say is that they are learning communication and from this starting point there are many ways to go. But there are so many jobs only available for people who can also market. There are so many companies who require additional marketing skills — although they don't know that they require this and they don't know what to call these skills because they don't really know how to go about marketing globally. So, we've incorporated technical writing into the programme and what I'd really like to do is incorporate more business courses into it.

Kirsten Malmkjaer: Could I ask you what categories you use? I think your examples are great and very interesting, but if you want to teach people how to write communicative texts and how to translate I would have thought it useful to have certain general categories. In your paper you talk about the link between theory and training and you mention Peirce's semiotics. Is that something you use in your training?

Peter Newmark: I think Peirce is too marginal for the kind of work a translator does. Also, teaching the translation of advertising is best suited to a special short course. You couldn't really incorporate it into a basic translation course — there are thousands of other things you have to do.

Kirsten Malmkjaer: Well I'm not suggesting that you teach fully-fledged Peirce, because that's a hard thing at any level. But as the paper shows, the three categories, icon, index and symbol, seem to work quite well. It might be useful to explain them to students because it's a generalisation over the millions of individual difficulties and translation problems to a certain extent, but it's good to give students some more general ideas about this.

Beverly Adab: Indeed, Peirce's three concepts can help students to identify the type of error, rationalise choices and justify selection or rejection of alternatives, within the context of the communicative function of the message.

Candace Séguinot: This is something which frustrates me as a translation teacher, because as a language teacher, which is how I began, you have a pretty good indication that if you take a certain approach you're going to wind up with either fluency or accuracy. But with our translation programme — although individual units may have different objectives such as more documentation or more flexible skills — there isn't an indication that the programme will move people in a particular way. So there's no way of knowing that if, for example, you empower students they won't be inaccurate or pompous, whilst at the same time you have to teach them that translation is a service industry within a corporate hierarchy which could do a lot better if it had more vision. So, it's hard to know how to balance this.

Said Faiq: I think the main issue in training interpreters and translators is to prepare them and give them the skills to face whatever specific problem they come across. I can't imagine the translation graduate walking out of university with carrier bags full of translated texts and when the employer asks him/her to translate a text, they say excuse me, I'll look to see if I've ever done one of these before. Most translators I know actually went into certain expert areas by their own choosing. You won't find students opting for a degree in medical translation, for example, because they will think it's too specialised and they'll wonder what they're going to do with it afterwards. They want to be able to say that they have handled a wide range of texts during their course and that they feel confident to cope with the texts their employer gives them. So, what we should be aiming for is a more holistic approach which rotates around a sound theoretical input.

Rina Ben-Shahar (University of Haifa): I think we know that the training of translators is usually very language-centred, and it's not that you can prepare the student exactly for each single situation, that s/he would know exactly how to translate a specific phrase. But if we can enhance his/her awareness of semiotics, not only of language, then when they compare situations that occur in different cultures — for example, this notion of slimming — they have a repertoire in every culture and they can make the right choices. I think we are not sufficiently aware of this repertoire of models and sub-models through which we look at reality.

Said Faiq: I think that's why the training of translators needs to build up processing skills, so that, for instance, they are able to forget about the text and rewrite something else, to enable them to manoeuvre around and actually change things. Particularly in advertising, the linguistic norm is there to be violated in order to achieve certain pragmatic aims such as selling the product. At the end of the day, the translator too is a consumer who is affected by ads.

Heike Perry: We need to equip the student with the ideas of taking on a text and seeing the text as a manifold phenomenon and seeing what is to be done in the other culture in order to recreate the various aspects of that phenomenon with all its interdependent effects.

Said Faiq: Always keeping in mind that the text is the master.

Christina Schäffner: Translators and translation scholars working within the functionalist approach, for example Skopos Theory, would say the purpose is the master, the purpose decides about translation strategies and methods.

Kirsten Malmkjaer: That comes back to what I was saying about deconstructing the ad and recreating the ad, rather than translating the ad. Many people would argue that ads belong to a category which cannot be translated, but which in fact have to be rewritten, taking into account all these considerations which we've been talking about. For example, that translators should be empowered to not even use the same English if it doesn't go. So, if the aim of the ad is to sell a product then the ad should be recreated for this purpose.

Said Faiq: That's right, that's processing — being able to recreate, while keeping the spirit. At the end of the day, ads are instructive texts. They are instructing the customer to do something with the option of whether to do it or not. The actual purpose of the text is to minimise the number of options the receiver has.

Beverly Adab: But the hidden agenda or text function are constant and known to be so. What the translator has to recreate is the effect in terms of self-image and product image, in order to achieve the desired result. This is true re-creation.

Candace Séguinot: I'd like to make the point that it's quite dangerous to teach students that they can do this kind of re-creation with the same time constraints as for a translation. People work for months on an advertising campaign and to say to students that they have to come up with something gives them the idea that they can do without research — which is really silly — because they have to acquire the marketing skills. One of the dangers too of asking them to come up with something new is that they don't understand how much image costs. You can't give someone freedom without equipping them.

Christina Schäffner: This is also a question of how we define translation — what are translators doing and how much are they allowed to do? And how can they explain and justify, or even defend, what they are doing? We're past the stage where you learned translation by just doing a lot of translation. But then we have to ask what to teach? The answer could be problem solving strategies, finding answers to questions such as, what kind of text is this, what is its role in the source culture, for what is the text needed when it's translated, and to what purpose will it be put in the target culture? When you take all these factors into account, and you then come to the conclusion, for example, that you have to change the image, then it is still legitimate to call it translation.

The Role of Culture

Helen Kelly-Holmes: I wonder what the future of translation is in global advertising. I see two trends here: the trend towards producing highly targeted, culture-specific texts within particular cultures; and the trend towards global, acultural advertising with little or no language, appealing to the lowest common denominator of universal, feel-good images. So, I wonder where translation fits into this? Particularly since translators see themselves as transmitters of culture, whereas in the translation of advertising this is not the paramount issue — in fact quite the opposite.

Beverly Adab: Translators are in fact responsible, in many instances, for the creation or perpetuation of a global sub-culture, for the virtual elimination of inter-cultural differences across nations through an appeal to a global socio-economic culture. The increasing role of international mass media communications accelerates this trend.

Helen Kelly-Holmes: So is there value in translating an advertising concept which is specifically designed for one culture? Is it not more efficient in the long-run to devise different concepts for different cultures?

Paul Kußmaul: I feel that some recent translation theory relates exactly to what we've just been talking about. The traditional idea was that there was either translation or adaptation and now more recently the translator is supposed to be doing both things. For example, Skopos theory is based on the notion that you must consider the purpose first and the source text second. The source text is seen as a kind of offer of information. But in order to be able to apply this to translation practice, you need to have a very good knowledge of the target culture. I wonder how we could build a course of studies out of this and what aspects of culture we would have to teach. And, in particular, how can we teach popular culture with the aid of other sciences such as cultural anthropology?

Secondly, these cultural considerations are not just important in translating advertising. Another example is academic discourse which is also very culture-specific. There are different conventions in the Germanic and Anglo-Saxon traditions. And, if you want to have an effect on your reader, you must consider these conventions and traditions.

Candace Séguinot: There's a humanistic tradition in Europe and a behaviourist tradition in North America. An example of this difference is the translation of Freud. Many theorists feel the translation was not faithful to Freud, but if it had been, Freud's ideas would never have been accepted.

Peter Newmark: I think there's been an over-emphasis on going from one culture to another — although there is a great deal of this in translating advertising. Even items you touched on in your paper, travel literature, health, education, these are universal issues that go beyond culture. They're sometimes dressed in cultural clothes, but that's as far as it goes. Paul's point about the Anglo-Saxon versus the Germanic style of academic writing is far more a universal question of good writing versus this clouded kind of writing that you often get in academic articles. Just thinking of culture — although culture is important — is going to cloud the issue. If you want to get something across in an advertisement, you often do it in a simple kind of universal way and blow the local culture!

Beverly Adab: I was wondering to what extent in Canada you're experiencing the spread of a neutral global culture, where there are certain underlying mythologies and universals behind all messages and to what extent you can train translators to recognise those as well as the culture-specific ones. Also, to what extent are these universals translator-led or driven and to what extent is the translator dominated by them?

Said Faiq: In addition to this, I would like to relate the cultural issue to text. The actual first stop for a translator is the source text and a belief system is built around that text. This comes back to the pragmatic intentions behind the production of the text, that is, why the text was produced in the first instance. If translators can achieve this full understanding of the intention of the source text, then an appropriate rendering into the target language is possible.

Heike Perry: But surely the purpose of the target language text is more important. This is not always found in the source language text.

Candace Séguinot: This is true. The effect desired in the target language culture may not be the same as the one desired in the source language culture. Function and text type may change.

Said Faiq: But these are extras added on to the translation process.

Helen Kelly-Holmes: They're more than that. They're the context.

Peter Newmark: In the course of your paper you say that you wouldn't have an advertisement exploiting the desire for youth in a country that reveres age. Is this something you've learned from your own experience and is it really true?

Candace Séguinot: Well, I think this would be everybody's experience. And when translating advertising for countries such as China or India, the translator needs to be aware of a different cultural tradition and consequently a different attitude in respect to this.

Incorporating Translation into the Production Process

Peter Newmark: Another point you mentioned: you said in some agencies experts work alongside translators, and some translators actually have product specialisms. An ideal situation. But in reality, translators cannot reject assignments easily, even if they don't have access to the detailed information necessary to do the job properly.

Candace Séguinot: Could I counter Peter with a concrete example, I was sitting in a translator's office and someone called and wanted her to translate from English to French. The English came from the Danish. It was only two words, 'fish paste', and she rejected it and said if you want me to do this, send me a tube.

Christina Schäffner: This is very much the line taken by Justa Holz-Mänttäri in Finland. She says that you, as the translator, are the expert and that you are responsible for the quality. You can't give quality without access to all the information available. She never signs a contract unless she has a guarantee that she can talk to the producers, and that they will take her to the factory for example. And also she speaks of text production as translational acting rather than of translating a source text.

Geoffrey Samuelsson-Brown: As a technical translation agency, we're often faced with this dilemma. Quite often a product hasn't even been made and we have to translate the documentation. What do you do in a situation like that?

Margaret Rogers: There's another point here about insisting on seeing the product and that is if translation isn't planned properly into the production process, as it should be, then you're always going to be in that situation and you can't simply reject the job. The professional way of going about this is to plan the translation into the production process. Then you've suddenly got to deal with the fact that when you start translating you don't know what the end product is going to look like.

Geoffrey Samuelsson-Brown: Documentation is part of the product and has to be produced within the deadline. So, you either have to reject that assignment and lose the client or deal with it in the best way you can.

Candace Séguinot: Some manufacturers now go about documenting in a very different way. What they do is hire native-speaker technical writers and they all document at the same time, as opposed to going through translation and that makes sense. That's one of the reasons why we want to be able to train our students to do that.

Geoffrey Samuelsson-Brown: Fortunately there's now something called the European Community Machinery Directive which states that anything relating to health and safety, instructions for use etc., has to be in one of the accepted languages of the country to which the product is being exported. So this means that manufacturers now have to incorporate documentation as part of the product and, *ipso facto*, translation. But that's only in certain cases.

Margaret Rogers: One of the reasons why I think translation should be planned into the process and not left till the end is to avoid some of the pitfalls Candace pointed out, such as space and lay-out and the relationship of text to pictures and so on. All of these things are very important and it's often difficult and expensive to change them at the end. But if translation is planned at an early point in the production process, then the translator can do a much more professional job. It avoids the need for compromise right at the end of the process because nobody's thought about translation.

Geoffrey Samuelsson-Brown: So many companies give no thought at all to translation. I recently gave a presentation to a group of companies in Los Angeles, trying to persuade them to export to Europe. Because the size of the market is roughly equivalent to that in the USA, a lot of people there thought that everyone in Europe spoke English and there was no need for translation.

Candace Séguinot: This attitude is more prevalent than you might think. I attended a technical writers' conference where someone was trying to convince people that writing their texts in Esperanto would be fine!

Heike Perry: Often a problem for the translator is that the original text is not clear and sometimes doesn't make sense. I've had the experience myself and you have to insist on seeing the product in order to write a new text in the target language that clearly explains the features of the product.

Said Faiq: I'd like to ask Geoffrey whether his translators ever translate into a language that is not their native tongue?

Geoffrey Samuelsson-Brown: Only if the translation is strictly for informational purposes and the client knows that this is not the language of habitual use of the translator.

Peter Newmark: This is the normal situation in this country because we're in the privileged position of having English as our native language. But this is not always the case in other countries. Some people think it's immoral to translate into a non-native language, but sometimes it's necessary and so long as it can be checked by someone who has this as their language of habitual use what's wrong with it? I'm not going against what you said, I'm just pointing this out.

Mona Baker: Of course in Scandinavian countries you can't become a certified translator unless you can offer more than one language into which you can translate.

Candace Séguinot: We need to make a distinction between the ideal situation and the pragmatic decisions that need to be taken. We're fortunate enough to have a sufficient number of native speakers of English and French in Canada. But when I look at a country like Finland — not many native speakers of other languages learn Finnish. So in non-Eurocentric translation, the rules aren't the same.

Marrying the Academic and the Practical

Geoffrey Samuelsson-Brown: I'd like to make the point that translation companies have an obligation to train their staff because students come out of university and although they have their degree, without any practical experience or specialist knowledge, it's not of great use.

Beverly Adab: What exactly are you training them in — text types, functions, skills, strategies?

Geoffrey Samuelsson-Brown: Translation techniques. Somebody acts as their guide and mentor and can pass on experience so as to avoid the same mistakes being made again. And if these more senior colleagues have a particular specialism, they can pass on these skills to an interested trainee.

Peter Newmark: Is this also the case if they come from a postgraduate training course?

Geoffrey Samuelsson-Brown: I know that we're looking more and more for people with a basic language degree and postgraduate studies, particularly ones which include a placement.

Beverly Adab: What kind of problem-solving strategies are you looking for in your translators? And how would you define the term 'skill' in a commercial translation context?

Geoffrey Samuelsson-Brown: The ability to deal with translations in a commercial environment.

Beverly Adab: In terms of looking at units of sense, meaning segments or in terms of language pair strategies?

Mona Baker: Or perhaps something not related to language at all, for example the ability to deal with clients?

Geoffrey Samuelsson-Brown: Yes, in a sense. They have their academic skills from university and they need to learn commercial skills as well.

Christina Schäffner: Are your translators specialised in a particular subject area?

Geoffrey Samuelsson-Brown: We're trying to work towards that, but if we don't have the skills in-house, then we pass the job on to freelancers. It's a dilemma.

How do you learn to become a translator if you don't get practice, but should you really be doing jobs for which you don't have the skills?

Rachel Brough: I always tell our students that no matter how hard they may think their year with us is, they will learn more in their first three months in a company than on an academic course. So nobody should think that you come out clutching an MA and that's it.

Beverly Adab: This is true. You can't claim to teach anything beyond strategies which will equip students to deal with problem types, taking into account context and target text functions.

Margaret Rogers: I think it would be foolish to claim that even students who have spent four years obtaining linguistic and cultural skills, including a period of extended study abroad, and a one year post-graduate course are fully-fledged translators. I see that postgraduate year as an apprenticeship and then when they go into a company or work with other translators, that's akin to a germinating period, where they can work closely with colleagues who have broader experience and can advise them. I see what we do in our courses as an apprenticeship stage.

Mona Baker: I wanted to come back to the specific training implications of what Candace talked about in her paper — space limitations, legal differences etc. I wonder how these could be incorporated into components of a training programme and what areas this programme would have to cover in order to sensitise students to the problems of this particular type of translation.

Candace Séguinot: One of the things I use with the students is Roland Barthes' article *Pasta* in *Communications* which deals with a semiotic analysis of pasta and that works very well with our students. One of the problems with training is that the students haven't had much experience of life and you can't give them that! One student who was working in insurance made a big mistake because she didn't know what a beneficiary was — not the linguistic term itself, but she didn't understand how insurance works. And neither can we expect her to, she's not a consumer in the sense that we are consumers. The problem is not just about doing promotional material — I haven't even talked today about the language problems — but the students get trapped because they make mistakes like any consumer, because the hidden messages are hidden! So, once you train them to identify the marketing function, you can train them to watch for the traps. For example, when translating the French 'mathematically proven', they opt for the collocation they know best which is 'statistically proven', which has a very different legal meaning. So you need to train them to step back and look at what happens with any kind of promotional language.

Mona Baker: That covers the politics of promotional language, but there are other areas you mentioned earlier and in your paper.

Candace Séguinot: The problem with translation is that there is no real solution, just options, and in addition there are usually time constraints. Quite often, you could do things with a text if you had the time. So you also have to teach students the importance of managing their time — something which has to be learned experientially.

I'm not for classification, I'm much more for skill-building. If you teach a course which is text- or genre-oriented, then you don't get into anything Paul Kußmaul was talking about — that is, the whole notion of purpose.

Educating the Public and Improving the Status of Translation

Kirsten Malmkjaer: I think we have a problem at the moment in Britain in that I think the Government is going to withdraw funding for MA courses in trans-lation. Translation really has to struggle to get itself recognised. This also has to do with the way we are currently assessed at British universities. There's a lot of documentation about what the aims of the course are and how these are going to be achieved and maybe that's why people are so keen to talk about strategies and course components today. I don't know if this is also the situation in Canada?

Candace Séguinot: I don't know whether it's fortunate or unfortunate, but we seem to be in a position where we do not have to do this in the universities, although there is an obligation to do so in the community colleges, which are roughly equivalent to your former polytechnics. But it's still uncertain where the cuts will fall and we still have to provide valid reasons for offering translation rather than units of psychology or linguistics. We also have to justify the number of staff we need by arguing that translation is a discipline.

Paul Kußmaul: It's only really in the last three decades that translation has come to be recognised as a separate discipline. And it still isn't well enough established. It does not have high prestige and so it's always affected by cut-backs. This was one of the reasons for founding the European Society for Translation Studies in order to make the public aware that there is a field of research and training called translation. But it's a slow process.

Heike Perry: Do you do anything to re-educate, as it were, the consumers of translation services so that they become more aware of the problems translators face and the information they need?

Candace Séguinot: I go and talk to professional organisations. For example, I gave a lecture to the Society of Technical Writers on how to write documentation with multinational translation in mind. And when I've highlighted to them all the problems translators face because of the way these texts are written, they come away with a new understanding and respect for the work of the translator. So we do see educating the public as part of our role.

Peter Newmark: Surely you have no need to. The situation in Canada couldn't be more different than it is in this country. Is there not a much greater awareness of translation among the general public?

Candace Séguinot: We're much better off, yes. But there are still problems. One of the problems of going back to the culture is the difference between using a model to reproduce something and being given a license to create something new.

Geoffrey Samuelsson-Brown: The translator has got to learn to ask questions not just about the product, but also about the text, its function, target group etc. If you don't look for this, you can't do a decent translation.

Said Faiq: But we also have to create some sort of ethics of translation because the client can always go to some other translator who will do the job more quickly for less money without asking questions.

Rachel Brough: I disagree with what you said about clients not wanting the translator to ask questions. I have clients who prefer to work with me because I ask questions and they're suspicious of translators who don't because there's a danger that something is being glossed over.

Mike Grover (Multilingual Matters): But you're dealing with an educated client. You have to show the client that the translation will cost more, but that a bad translation will cost even more in the long run.

Candace Séguinot: Technical writers are very fortunate because in recent years they've become much more involved in the whole production process. So it's more acceptable for them to be involved as representatives of how people think and so they have an impact on design and conception. But I don't see this happening in translation. Maybe the fact that technical writers are now called technical communicators or information developers has helped their status. As technical translators, we should also strive for a similar type of recognition and for the integration of our role into the whole production and marketing process.